"This book is the perfect complement to Tripp's *Dangerous Calling*. The warning of 'functional gospel amnesia' captures so well why this book is needed. Leaders do not need more gimmicks. Leaders need more grace. They need more gospel."

Daniel L. Akin, President, Southeastern Baptist Theological Seminary

"The strength of this book lies in the way Tripp shapes his treatment of leadership by two things: his understanding of the gospel, and his grasp of the organic nature of the local church. At one level, this is an easy read; at another level, it is sometimes probing and painful."

D. A. Carson, Emeritus Professor of New Testament, Trinity Evangelical Divinity School; Cofounder, The Gospel Coalition

"Tripp knows the heart and hurts of the leader. He writes with a vulnerable compassion borne out of shared experiences and a conviction rooted in deep biblical wisdom. *Lead* is by far the best book on ministry leadership I have read and one to which I will undoubtedly return."

Mark Bailey, President and Senior Professor of Bible Exposition, Dallas Theological Seminary

"Wow. I had no idea that reviewing this book would become so very personal, so penetrating—an experience of leadership surgery that sliced my soul open with conviction and then sutured it shut with grace. Tripp is among the few who have the experience, stature, transparency, and clarity to call church leaders back to the urgency of gospel transformation in ministry. May God give me, and all of us, ears to hear these truths . . . and enough courageous humility to apply them!"

Dave Harvey, President, Great Commission Collective; author, *I Still Do*

"While this book is written primarily for pastors and ministry leaders, it is appropriate for any Christ-following leaders who operate in the sacred or the secular. As a leader who spent thirty years in c-suite roles in business and now almost four years as a leader in a global ministry, I found the twelve gospel principles to be spot on. I encourage any leader, either in business or ministry, to pick this book up and digest it."

Steve Shackelford, Chief Executive Officer, Redeemer City to City

"Only read this book if you are desperate to be a more humble, gentle, and gracious servant of Christ. If you want something that will chart your way to ecclesiastical fame and celebrity-pastor status, this is not it. This book is about sacrificial, humble, death-to-self leadership—not self-centered, superficial, self-promoting, narcissistic authoritarianism. On every page, Tripp challenges us to recapture a thoroughly biblical approach to leadership in the church, and that is precisely what we need as we lead amid the raging battle all around us—a battle for our joy, our perseverance, our lives, our families, and for the people we serve—to the end that God would get all the glory, and not us."

Burk Parsons, Senior Pastor, Saint Andrew's Chapel, Sanford, Florida; Editor, *Tabletalk*

"Tripp's books have been some of the most influential in my life. *Lead* is no exception! You will find within the pages of this book practical, gospel-centered help as you lead and serve others."

Jennie Allen, *New York Times* best-selling author, *Get Out of Your Head*; Founder, IF:Gathering

I think I have read everything Paul Tripp has written! Few people have inspired and instructed me with clear, gospel-saturated wisdom like he has, and I'm excited to see him apply this wisdom to leadership. As is often said, everything rises or falls on leadership, including the family, the home, and the spiritual self. *Dangerous Calling* was eerily prophetic in its anticipation of the fall of a number of high-profile leaders, each one adding to the heartbreak of a church in a leadership crisis. I am grateful to see that conversation extended, and I hope many will not only read this book, but saturate themselves in the gospel it puts forward."

—**J. D. Greear,** President, Southern Baptist Convention; author, *Not God Enough*; Pastor, The Summit Church, Raleigh-Durham, North Carolina

LEAD

Other books by Paul David Tripp

A Quest for More: Living for Something Bigger Than You

Age of Opportunity: A Biblical Guide for Parenting Teens (Resources for Changing Lives)

Awe: Why It Matters for Everything We Think, Say, and Do

Broken-Down House: Living Productively in a World Gone Bad

Come, Let Us Adore Him: A Daily Advent Devotional

Dangerous Calling: Confronting the Unique Challenges of Pastoral Ministry

Forever: Why You Can't Live without It

Grief: Finding Hope Again

How People Change (with Timothy S. Lane)

Instruments in the Redeemer's Hands: People in Need of Change Helping People in Need of Change (Resources for Changing Lives)

Journey to the Cross: A 40-Day Lenten Devotional

Lost in the Middle: Midlife and the Grace of God

My Heart Cries Out: Gospel Meditations for Everyday Life

New Morning Mercies: A Daily Gospel Devotional

Parenting: 14 Gospel Principles That Can Radically Change Your Family

Redeeming Money: How God Reveals and Reorients Our Hearts

Sex in a Broken World: How Christ Redeems What Sin Distorts

Shelter in the Time of Storm: Meditations on God and Trouble

Suffering: Eternity Makes a Difference (Resources for Changing Lives)

Suffering: Gospel Hope When Life Doesn't Make Sense

Teens and Sex: How Should We Teach Them? (Resources for Changing Lives)

War of Words: Getting to the Heart of Your Communication Struggles (Resources for Changing Lives)

What Did You Expect?: Redeeming the Realities of Marriage

Whiter Than Snow: Meditations on Sin and Mercy

LEAD

Paul David Tripp

CROSSWAY®
WHEATON, ILLINOIS

Lead

Copyright © 2020 by Paul David Tripp

Published by Crossway
1300 Crescent Street
Wheaton, Illinois 60187

Cover Image and Design: Ordinary Folk, ordinaryfolk.co

First printing 2020

Printed in the United States of America

Unless otherwise indicated, Scripture quotations are from the ESV® Bible (The Holy Bible, English Standard Version®), copyright © 2001 by Crossway, a publishing ministry of Good News Publishers. Used by permission. All rights reserved.

All emphases in Scripture quotations have been added by the author.

Hardcover ISBN: 978-1-4335-6763-6
ePub ISBN: 978-1-4335-6766-7
PDF ISBN: 978-1-4335-6764-3
Mobipocket ISBN: 978-1-4335-6765-0

Library of Congress Cataloging-in-Publication Data

Names: Tripp, Paul David, 1950- author.
Title: Lead : 12 gospel principles for leadership in the church / Paul David Tripp.
Description: Wheaton, Illinois : Crossway, 2020. | Includes indexes.
Identifiers: LCCN 2019041183 (print) | LCCN 2019041184 (ebook) | ISBN 9781433567636 (hardcover) | ISBN 9781433567643 (pdf) | ISBN 9781433567650 (mobipocket) | ISBN 9781433567667 (epub)
Subjects: LCSH: Christian leadership.
Classification: LCC BV652.1 .T755 2020 (print) | LCC BV652.1 (ebook) | DDC 253–dc23
LC record available at https://lccn.loc.gov/2019041183
LC ebook record available at https://lccn.loc.gov/2019041184

Crossway is a publishing ministry of Good News Publishers.

LSC		31	30	29	28	27	26	25	24	23	22	21
14	13	12	11	10	9	8	7	6	5	4	3	2

To all the leaders who invested in me, shepherded me, confronted me, prayed for me, and modeled for me the patient, forgiving, transforming grace of my Savior.

CONTENTS

PREFACE

IT IS ONE OF THE DISTINCT, undeserved privileges and joys of my life. I did not train to do it, did not see it coming, and continue to carry the surprise with me to this day. I have been called to put gospel words on page after page after page in book after book. I get up each morning with enthusiasm and appreciation. At first, writing did not come naturally to me. I wrote with about as much confidence as a person, swept into the winter spirit, ice skating for the first time. My first manuscript came back with the editor's corrections and comments in red, and it looked like a botched transfusion! But I've kept at it and am so deeply grateful that this is what I get to do with my life, my time, my gifts, and my knowledge.

I only have one thing to offer: the right-here, right-now truths of the gospel of the Lord Jesus Christ. All I ever do with each book is put on my gospel glasses and look at another topic in the life of a believer or in the culture of the church. I have jokingly said that I have written only one book; I just retitle it every year. Because the gospel is so infinitely deep, I know I could keep digging into it for the next century and never reach the bottom. I also know that applications of the gospel to everyday life are so wide and varied that I would also never run out of new things to examine from a gospel perspective.

You see, the gospel is not just a set of historical facts. It is that, for sure. It is rooted in divine acts of intervention and substitution that if not real and historical would rob the gospel of its reliability, promise, and power. But the gospel is not just a set of historical facts; it is also a collection of present redemptive realities. Certain things are true now, and are true of every believer, because of what God historically did and is presently doing on their behalf. There is more. The gospel is a living identity for all who believe. We have become something in Christ, something that is glorious and new and filled with new potential. Good gospel theology doesn't just define for you who God is and what he has done; it also redefines who you are as his child.

There is one final thing. As I said earlier, the gospel is meant to be a new set of glasses that every believer wears and through which he looks at life. Let me say it another way. The gospel of Jesus Christ is meant to be your life hermeneutic, that is, the means by which you understand and make sense of life. This is important because human beings don't live life based on the facts of their experience but on their interpretation of the facts. Whether they are aware of it or not, every human being is a meaning maker, a theologian, a philosopher, or an anthropologist, always taking things apart to understand what they mean. As a ministry leader, you are doing theological work not just when you preach, teach, or lead but also in the ways that you think about yourself, understand your ministry, and relate to fellow leaders. Every book I write is written to help people look at some aspect of life or ministry through the lens of the gospel.

Sometimes this wonderful work I have been given is easy and flows fluidly; the words seem to fly out of my fingers and onto the page. But other times I seem to spend a lot of my writing time looking at the unwritten page, debating how things would be best said and praying for wisdom and ability that I do not have on my own. On those days, I'm not sure how much of it is me and the variety of distractions and weaknesses that I bring to the writing process or if it is the topic and all the delicate balances that need to be expressed well. I am not discouraged when the work is hard, because I am deeply convinced that I have been called to do this work—not first because I am glorious in gift and wisdom but because my Lord is glorious in every way, and he meets me in my weakness with strength that only he can give.

I write always as a pastor. This may seem strange to you, but I write with a congregation in view in my mind's eye. I write with love for the people in view. I write with a passion for them to know the full depth and breadth of what they have been given in the amazing grace and boundless love of Jesus. And I know that because the work of Jesus on our behalf is so completely sufficient, I can be honest. There is no damage that sin has done or will do that hasn't been addressed by his person, work, promises, and presence. I write convinced that we, the community of believers, can be the most honest community on earth because there is nothing that could be known, revealed, or exposed about us that hasn't been covered by Christ's atoning work.

In the end, I trust that my work will not just give people a new way to think about the gospel information that they find in their Bibles but will ultimately lead to heart and life transformation. I write with the hope that my words will stimulate faith, love, hope, courage, joy, humility, perseverance, mercy, and generosity, and that these things will live not only in all the typical places where people live and relate but also in the relationships and work of those commissioned to give leadership to the church.

It is with these hopes that I offer this book to you. I write as a pastor who loves pastors and has a deep appreciation and respect for the daily sacrifices that every ministry leader makes for the sake of the gospel of Jesus Christ and the spiritual health of the people of God. Like every other book I have written, I think of it as a gospel book. It is not first a ministry leadership critique but rather a call to let the gospel of Jesus Christ form the way we think of ourselves as leaders, the way we relate to one another as a leadership community, and the way we go about doing our ministry leadership work. This has not been an easy book, because I wrote wanting to examine hard things, but I do so in a way that reflects the hope and love of the gospel. I didn't want the honesty to diminish the hope or the hope to weaken the honesty. My hope is that as you read, you will be blessed not only with hope but hope that corrects, protects, and sets a new agenda where needed.

May God richly bless you and all you do in his name!

Paul David Tripp
May 13, 2019

INTRODUCTION

Crisis

I LOVE THE CHURCH. I love its worship, I love its preaching, I love its gospel theology, I love its community, I love its witness to the world, I love its ministries of mercy, and I love its leaders. When I have the privilege of standing before a gathering of church leaders, I am always filled with a deep sense of honor and appreciation. I know well the road that every pastor travels because I have walked that long road myself. I know the burden of being a member of the core shepherding and leadership community of the church. I have the highest respect for those who answer the call to give their life to church ministry. I know the average pastor is overworked, understaffed, and underpaid, so I have such appreciation for those who have chosen to live that life. I am a member of a wonderful church, with godly and dedicated leadership and life-giving gospel preaching. Being part of its community is one of the joys of my life.

The love that I have for the church is why I am concerned for the leaders of the church. My concern has deepened as I have gotten call after call, calls that have come as a result of my book *Dangerous*

Calling.[1] The particular call that follows came from the head of a local church board with which I had a loose ministry partnership. He was shocked, hurt, angry, and confused. He called for my help, but I'm not sure he wanted my help, at least not the help that I felt constrained to give him. It wasn't long into the conversation that his anger turned toward me. I wanted to help him and his band of fellow leaders through the dark and rocky road that they would walk over the next several months, but his anger told me I wouldn't be invited in. I put down my cell phone after our talk and sadness washed over me. It wasn't the first time, and I knew it wouldn't be the last. I carry that sadness with me. It drives me to prayer, it makes me celebrate God's grace, and it motivates me to think that we can and we must do better.

What concerned me with the call that day and many other similar calls is not that my leader friend was shocked, hurt, and angry. He should have been shocked at the duplicitous life of the senior pastor he was calling about. He should have been hurt that his pastor loved his pleasure more than he loved the people he'd been called to feed and to lead. The caller needed to be righteously angry at the violation of everything God designed his church to be. But what concerned me and left me sad after the call was that there was no introspection, no wonderment about the nature of the leadership community that surrounded the fallen pastor, and no apparent willingness to talk about things other than what to do with the pastor who was the focus of his anger.

I wish this conversation had been an exception, but it wasn't. We have all been witnesses to the fall of well-known pastors with a huge amount of influence and notoriety, but for every public falling, there are hundreds of unknown pastors who have lapsed, have left both their leadership and their church in crisis, or are

---

1. Paul David Tripp, *Dangerous Calling: Confronting the Unique Challenges of Pastoral Ministry* (Wheaton, IL: Crossway, 2012).

spiritual shells of the pastors they once were. We have talked about the idolatry of celebrity, about pastoral immorality, and about seduction of power, but I am writing this book because, very often, behind the failure of a pastor is a weak and failed leadership community. We don't have just a pastoral crisis; I am convinced from conversation after conversation with pastors and their leadership that we have a *leadership crisis.*

Could it be that the way we have structured local church leadership, the way leaders relate to one another, the way we form a leader's job description, and the everyday lifestyle of the leadership community may be contributing factors to pastoral failure? Could it be that as we leaders are disciplining the pastor, dealing with the hurt he has left behind and working toward restoration, we need to look inward and examine what his fall tells us about ourselves? Could it be that we are looking to the wrong models to understand how to lead? Could it be that as we have become enamored with corporate models of leadership, we have lost sight of deeper gospel insights and values? Could it be that we have forgotten that the call to lead Christ's church is not summarized by organizing, running, and funding a weekly catalog of religious gatherings and events? Could it be that many of our leadership communities don't actually function like communities? And could it be that many of our leaders don't really want to be led, and many in our leadership community don't value true biblical community?

I knew when I wrote *Dangerous Calling*, which addresses the unique temptations that every pastor faces, I would need to write another book addressing the community of leaders that surrounds the pastor. I have needed the years since *Dangerous Calling* was published, with all of those sad and difficult phone conversations, before undertaking it. I have needed to sit face-to-face with scores of pastoral newbies and veterans. I have needed many hours of examination and reflection. But I am excited to use my voice in the hope that it will ignite a conversation that I am convinced we need to have but often are not having.

This book is not a depressing critique. You can go to Twitter for that—the place that has revealed to us all that judgment is much more natural to us than grace. I want to propose a positive character model for local church or ministry leadership. There is so much written about a leader's gifting, about having the right people in the right seats, about leadership structures, and about how to make decisions and drive vision. All of these things are important, but they are not the most important thing. I want to turn your thinking toward the foundational character and lifestyle of a healthy church leadership community. My hope is that the result will be insight, confession, and community transformation.

Jim called me because the secret, sordid life of his senior pastor was no longer a secret. Like so many situations, the computer was the tool that had exposed the secret. At first, Jim and his fellow leaders were in denial. They simply could not believe that this stuff was going on in the life of the man they had worked alongside and trusted for years. They thought maybe his computer had been hacked, but when they approached him, they changed their thinking, because he had a denier's answer for everything. Now they had to work through their disbelief as well as all the plausible explanations their pastor had given and that, frankly, they wanted to believe. The more they dug, however, the more they were unable to deny the truth of what was uncovered, and the more they uncovered, the more they had to confess that there was an awful lot about this pastor that they did not know. They were like ten people in a canoe built for four launched by raging rapids toward a waterfall ahead.

To add to their out-of-control feeling, this crisis had shattered their unity. Perhaps it's more accurate to say that the crisis had exposed how thin and easily shatterable their unity was. The men who were most loyal to the pastor argued and debated with the men they thought were rushing to judgment; the organizational guys argued with the men who tended to be more pastoral; and in all of these debates there was way too much judgment of the others' interests and motives. Meanwhile, a shocked and hurting congregation was not getting from their leaders what they needed.

As I walked with these leaders through their distress and confusion, engaging them in conversation after conversation, it was clear that they were foundationally unprepared for what they were dealing with. It wasn't just that they were structurally unprepared; they were, more importantly, unprepared in terms of character and relationship. The fact that such basic things were missing complicated and obstructed their calling to lead their church through that very difficult moment. And in their unpreparedness, they spent as much time debating among themselves as they did dealing with the crisis and the man at the center of it.

It's not just the little, unknown churches that are unprepared. We have all watched flagship churches deal with similar pastoral crises, and we have seen them act and speak too soon, only to then retract what they have said and done and then suggest another view and another course of action that they soon also modify. We've seen leaders in these churches publicly disagree with one another. We have seen loyalty, power, and division control decisions rather than biblical wisdom. How many failed pastors will there be, how many more broken and hurting churches, before we humbly ask questions about how we are leading the church that the Savior has entrusted into our care?

I celebrate the wonderful, vibrant, and healthy churches that I partner with around the world. I love the energy that we are pouring into church planting and church revitalization. I love that gospel-centered churches are speaking ever more loudly as advocates for what is just and right for those who have no voice. I am not at all depressed; I am excited. But I am concerned that weaknesses in the leadership community have the power to not only weaken the function and witness of what appears to be a very healthy church but may also, in what seems to be an instant, cast that church into a quagmire that can damage and divert its ministry for a long time. In some situations it appears that the glory will never return.

The courage that propels me to approach this topic is rooted not in my wisdom or experience but in the presence, power, wisdom, and grace of my Redeemer. As I begin writing this book, I am once again remembering what gave me hope and motivation when I wrote *Dangerous Calling*—Matthew 28:16–20:

> Now the eleven disciples went to Galilee, to the mountain to which Jesus had directed them. And when they saw him they worshiped him, but some doubted. And Jesus came and said to them, "All authority in heaven and on earth has been given to me. Go therefore and make disciples of all nations, baptizing them in the name of the Father and of the Son and of the Holy Spirit, teaching them to observe all that I have commanded you. And behold, I am with you always, to the end of the age."

The disciples had been through a whirlwind of unimaginable things; the late-night arrest of their Messiah in Gethsemane, Jesus's trial and torture, the public crucifixion, the sight of his empty tomb and his post-resurrection appearances. Try to put yourself in their place. Try to imagine the confusion, the internal debates, the fear, the doubt, and the wonderment of the future. Imagine the joy of his appearances crashing against the struggles of belief that would accompany the miracles and the mystery. Consider what happens next in the context of what the disciples were dealing with emotionally and spiritually.

Jesus, knowing that there was both doubt and belief in the room, was about to commission this group of fearful believers to carry the gospel of resurrection life to the world. Yes, he would commission these men at this cataclysmic moment. I likely would've thought, *They're not ready, it's just too soon. They need to know so much more. They need to come to a deeper understanding of what just happened. They need time to mature.* But in the middle of the most amazing, confusing, and gloriously mind-bending moment in history, Jesus did not hesitate; he simply said, "Go."

I love the words that follow because they tell us why Jesus was confident to draft these men, at that moment, for his worldwide gospel mission. He was confident not because of what was in them and what he knew they would do, but because he knew what was in himself and what he would do. So he said, "All authority in heaven and on earth has been given to me." He was saying to these men that there was no situation, no location, or no community outside of his authority and sovereign rule. He wanted them to understand that everything in heaven and on earth was under his command. Consider why this was so vital for these men who desperately needed his grace in order to bring his message of grace to the nations.

I don't know if you've ever considered this, but the reliability of God's promises of grace to us is only as great as the extent of his sovereignty. God can only guarantee the sure delivery of his promises in the places over which he has control. I can guarantee what I promise to you in my house, because I have some authority there, but I cannot make the same promises for my neighbor's house, over which I have no control. Jesus is saying, "As you go, you can bank on everything I have promised you because I rule every place where you will need those promises to be fulfilled." God's promises of grace are sure because his sovereignty is complete.

But Jesus had more to say. He then looked at this room of men, with the mixture of doubt and faith in their hearts, and said, "Behold, I am with you always." These words are much deeper than Jesus saying, "I'll be there for you." Jesus is taking one of the names of God: "I Am." He says, "Know that wherever you go, the I Am will be with you, the God of Abraham, Isaac, and Jacob, the one on whom all the covenant promises rest, the one who is the same yesterday, today, and forever, the one who is Alpha and Omega. I am the I Am, and I would never think of sending you without going with you in power, glory, wisdom, and grace." The disciples would find all they needed for what they were being commissioned to do in the power, presence, and grace of the one sending them.

It is with the same assurance Jesus gave to the disciples that I write this book. Because of the completeness of Christ's authority, the inescapability of his presence and the surety of his promises, we don't have to be afraid of examining our weaknesses and failure. The gospel of his presence, power, and grace frees us from the burden of minimizing or denying reality. The gospel of his presence, power, and grace welcomes us to be the most honest community on earth. We are not cemented to our track record. We are not left to our small bag of personal resources. Because he is his best gift to us, our potential is great and change is possible. And so it is the gospel of his presence, power, and grace that gives me the courage and hope to write about a very important place where change needs to take place. May the same grace give you an open heart as you read.

A MODEL

The foundation of everything proposed in this book about the shape, character, and function of the leadership community of the church of Jesus Christ is this: the model for the community that is the church, and most importantly its leadership, is the gospel of Jesus Christ. Now, I know that this seems both obvious and vague, but I am persuaded that it is neither, and that if the primary driving force of leadership in local churches around the world was the gospel of Jesus Christ, many of the sad things we have seen happen in the lives of leaders and their churches would not have happened.

I want to invite you to examine with me a passage that lays down a gospel foundation for all relationships in the church, from the average person in the pew to the most influential, culture, and mission-setting leaders. Let me say, before we look at this passage, that no organizational or achievement-oriented leadership model should overwhelm the values and call of the gospel as the core structural and functional model and identity for local church and Christian ministry leaders. As I have reflected upon this passage, my mind has gone to the thousands and thousands of pastors, ministry leaders, elder boards, and deacon boards around the world, and I have wondered if the community norms of this passage are their normal experience as leaders. The passage comes in Paul's letter to the Ephesians:

> I therefore, a prisoner for the Lord, urge you to walk in a manner worthy of the calling to which you have been called, with all humility and gentleness, with patience, bearing with one another in love, eager to maintain the unity of the Spirit in the bond of peace. (Eph. 4:1–3)

It should be noted that Paul's first application of the truths of the gospel, which he has just expounded for the Ephesians, is to remind them that it is those very truths that are to form the way they think about themselves and their relationships to one another. Those truths are to be the foundation stones of whatever community structures they build. There are few more important applications of the truths of the gospel of Jesus Christ than to consider how they set the agenda for the way we live with, relate to, and work with each other as members of the body of Christ. And let me point out that there is no exception clause for pastors, elders, and deacons or some different community model for them in this passage or in any of the similar passages. The gospel, which is our hope in life and death, also sets the agenda for how we live, relate, and lead between the "already" of our conversion and the "not yet" of our final home going.

My purpose here is not to do a detailed study of Ephesians 4:1–3 but to propose how its gospel values can begin to form the way we think about how we function and relate as church leaders. I want to suggest that if you really do want your relationships to be worthy of the gospel you received, then you will value humility, gentleness, patience, forbearing love, and peace, and if you value these gospel characteristics, you will ask yourself, "What would my leadership community look like if we truly valued these things more than positions, power, achievement, acclaim, or success?" Let me answer this question by suggesting six characteristics that will mark out a leadership community formed by gospel values.

1. Humility

Humility means that each leader's relationship to other leaders is characterized by an acknowledgment that he deserves none of the recognition, power, or influence that his position affords him. It means knowing, as a leader, that as long as sin still lives inside you, you will need to be rescued from you. Humility means you love serving more than you crave leading. It means owning your inability rather than boasting in your abilities. It means always being committed to listen and learn. Humility means seeing fellow leaders not so much as serving your success but serving the one who called each of you. It means being more excited about your fellow leaders' commitment to Christ than you are about their loyalty to you. It's about fearing the power of position rather than craving it. It's about being more motivated to serve than to be seen. Humility is always being ready to consider the concern of others for you, confess what God reveals through them, and to commit to personal change. Humility is about firing your inner lawyer and opening yourself up to the ongoing power of transforming grace.

2. Dependency

Dependency means living, as a leader, as if I really do believe that my walk with God is a community project. It means that because of the blinding power of remaining sin, I give up on the belief that no one knows me better than I know myself. Dependency means no longer being afraid of exposure, because I really do believe that there is nothing that could be known, exposed, or revealed about me that has not already been addressed by the person and work of Jesus. It means living as if I really do believe that isolated, individualized, independent Christianity never produces good fruit. It means acknowledging that every leader needs to be led and every pastor needs to be pastored. Dependency means acknowledging theological understanding, biblical literacy, ministry gifts, and ministry experience and success do not mean that I no longer need the essential sanctifying ministry of the body of Christ. It means confessing that as long as sin remains in me, and that apart from restraining grace and the rescuing ministry of those around me, I continue to be a danger to myself.

3. Prepared Spontaneity

If you acknowledge the presence and the seducing and deceiving power of remaining sin, you will also acknowledge that everyone in your leadership community is still susceptible to temptation and is still at risk. You know that sins, small and great, will infect your community and obstruct and divert its work. You live with the knowledge that everyone in your leadership community is still in need of rescuing and sanctifying grace. So you set in motion plans for dealing with the sin, weakness, and failure that will inevitably rear their ugly heads. You will not be shocked by, deny, or minimize what God, in grace, reveals but deal with it forthrightly in a spirit of biblical love and grace. You will not be more concerned with defending the reputation of your leadership community than dealing with its failures. Prepared spontaneity means that because you have taken seriously what the gospel says about ongoing spiritual battles in the heart of every leader, you have prepared yourself to deal with the sin that God exposes, even though you don't know beforehand what he will, in grace, expose.

4. Inspection

Inspection means that we invite people to step over the normal boundaries of leadership relationships to look into our lives to help us see things that we would not see on our own. It means inviting fellow leaders to watch for our souls. It means inviting them to interrupt our private conversation with protective biblical insights and restorative gospel truths. It means acknowledging that self-examination is a community project, because we are still able to swindle ourselves into thinking that we are okay when we are in danger and in need of help. So every leader must be willing to live under loving, grace-infused, patient, and forgiving biblical inspection.

5. Protection

We all sin, but we don't all sin the same. For reasons of history, experience, gift, biology, and a host of other things, we aren't equally tempted by the same things. You may be susceptible to the temptations of power, while someone else may be susceptible to the temptations of pleasure, while I may be tempted by the lure of material things. This understanding of the variegated seductions of sin and the different way they impact each one of us is vital to the long-term health and gospel fruitfulness of every local church leadership community. True biblical love doesn't just accept you, bless you with patience, and greet your failures with forgiveness. Along with all these things, it works to do everything it can to protect you from the eternal weaknesses of heart that make you susceptible to temptation.

The words of Hebrews 13:17 speak with a motivational clarity: "Obey your leaders and submit to them, for they are keeping watch over your souls, as those who will have to give an account." Leaders are responsible to protect the souls of those who are under their care. The words here are both specific and provocative. It doesn't say leaders are commissioned to take note of your behavior; of course that is true, but there is something deeper and more fundamental pictured here. It's souls that leaders are held accountable to protect. *Soul* points to the inner person, his thoughts, desires, motives, weaknesses, strengths, level of maturity, susceptibilities, etc. It means knowing someone at the level of his heart so that you can predict where he may step over God's wise boundaries. What is depicted here is a level of protective leadership that will only ever happen in the context of depth of relationship.

If this protection is meant to be the experience of everyone in the body of Christ, should it not be present in the core leadership community? It has saddened me how many times I have been contacted to help a leadership community deal with a fallen leader, only to discover there were indicators all along of particular weakness and susceptibilities that no one in his leadership community seemed to see. Because we as leaders don't always see ourselves with accuracy, and because we don't always see the areas in which we are weak, we all need a protective community that is watching for us even when we aren't as watchful as we should be. If we are to be protected, we need to be known at the level where temptation is its most powerful, the heart.

6. Restoration

One of the most beautiful, hopeful, and encouraging gospel themes that courses its way through Scripture is the theme of fresh starts and new beginnings. Fresh starts and new beginnings are a hallmark of the rescuing, forgiving, restoring, and transforming power of God's grace. For Moses a fresh start looked like a burning-bush voice calling him back to Egypt to liberate God's people, this time by God's power. For David it meant being confronted by a prophet, confessing the horror of what he had done, and continuing his kingship. For Jonah it meant being vomited up on the seashore and commissioned a second time to take God's message to Nineveh. For Peter a fresh start happened on the shore of the Sea of Galilee, as the Messiah he betrayed forgave him and sent him once again into his service. For Paul, a fresh start and new beginning looked like a blinding light on a road to Damascus and words of forgiveness and commission carried by a rather fearful messenger.

Grace means we are not held to our worst moment or cursed by our worst decision. Grace means out of the ashes of sin, leaders can rise because the Savior has resurrection power. I wonder, in the way we think about leaders and the function of the leadership community, would we have restored any of these biblical characters? What is different about the way we look at the sin, weakness, and failure of a leader and the way God looks at the same? In none of the instances that I cited was the sin denied, hidden, or minimized. In each situation it looks as though what was done was so grave that there could be no hope for the sinner's future. Our tendency in such situations is to think that while God's forgiveness demonstrates amazing grace, he will nevertheless say, "As far as usefulness in my kingdom, you're done." But in those biblical situations, each was restored to a position of spiritual leadership.

I am going to have much more to say about this in a chapter to follow, but what I want to ask here is, Do our leadership communities function with a gospel-driven, restoration mentality? I know so many fallen leaders who were cast away and are supporting their families doing telemarketing, house construction, or computer sales. We should never minimize a leader's sin, nor should we rush to put a leader back in the saddle who has not yet dealt with central issues in his heart, and certainly there are some cases in which a leader should never be restored to a position of leadership, but we also must not abandon our functional belief in the restorative power of God's right-here, right-now grace.

The church is in desperate need of a leadership community whose function is not just structured to achieve with efficiency but is more deeply shaped by the comforts and calls of the gospel of Jesus Christ. As in every other relationship of human life, if you look at your leadership community through the lens of the gospel of Jesus Christ, it will transform your expectations, your commitments, your behavior, and the way you respond to difficulty. It is not just nebulous biblical talk to say that the gospel must be our model for the formation and function of the leadership community that is to guide the church. The focus of this book is the specific call of the gospel on the way we think about leadership.

TWELVE GOSPEL PRINCIPLES

I meet individually on a regular basis with ten young pastors and ministry leaders. There is nothing in ministry more important to me than this, and there are few things that I enjoy in ministry more. There is a real way in which these men are my ministry heroes. They have given their lives to live in the trenches in the middle of the spiritual battle that is the church. They deal with the full range of joys and hardships that are inevitable in ministry. They have been called, like their Messiah, not only to preach the gospel but also, like him, to suffer for its sake. I love walking with them through the twisted roads, the hills and valleys, and the shiny days and stormy nights of the life of a spiritual leader. But again and again I am saddened that they lack the kind of gospel-rich community that every pastor or leader needs in order to be spiritually healthy and to enjoy ministry longevity. My meetings with them have forced me to think about what that community needs to be like.

So this book is shaped by twelve leadership-community gospel principles. These principles are deeply relational because the gospel is. Remember that the gospel of God's grace teaches us that lasting change of heart and hands always takes place in the context of relationship, first with God and then with the people of God. One way that I think about the twelve principles that drive the content of this book is that they are a love letter to these dear men whom I walk with and have such affection for. My hope is that not only would these principles protect them and bless them with a long and healthy ministry life, but that they would do the same for you and generations of Christian leaders to come.

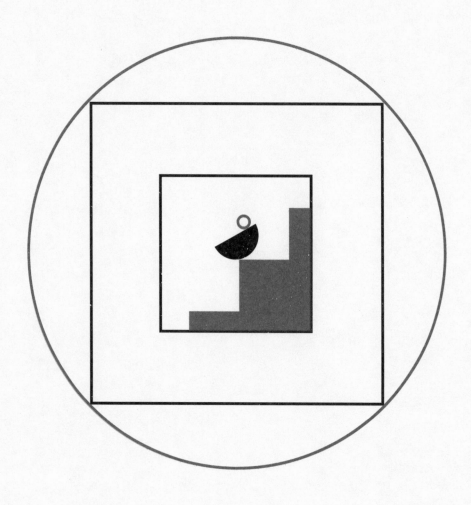

PRINCIPLE I

*A ministry community whose time is controlled by doing the
business of the church tends to be spiritually unhealthy.*

ACHIEVEMENT

EVERY LEADER LEADS while being in desperate personal need of the full resources of God's grace. This inescapable reality must be a major influence on the way those in the leadership community see themselves, conduct themselves, and do the work to which God has called them. It's not just the young pastor who needs grace or the struggling pastor or the fallen pastor; grace is the essential ingredient in the success of anyone's ministry, any time, at any age, in any location, and in any type of ministry.

The next chapter will unpack what it means for a leadership community to function like the gospel community that it was designed by God to be. In this chapter I want to consider how the good thing—achievement—can become a bad thing for leadership because it has become a ruling thing. Now, I know that achievement is not only a wonderful thing; it is also a vital thing. Salvation is all about achievement. There would be no hope of forgiveness, of present help, or of a new heavens and a new earth if it weren't for the unstoppable ambition of the Lord of lords to achieve what only he could achieve in extending his grace to his people and in redeeming and restoring his groaning world. But there is more.

God's saving grace ignites in the hearts of all his children a radical shift in ambition. Where once our thoughts, desires, words, and actions were motivated and directed by our ambition to achieve our definition of personal happiness, by grace they are now shaped by our ambition for the kingdom of God to achieve all God has designed for it to achieve. Where once we were ambitious for what we want, we now are ambitious to do the will of God. Further, God calls us to be ambitious for the growth and expansion of his kingdom between the "already" of our conversions and the "not yet" of our home going. Human beings are achievers, meant to build and rebuild, to grow and expand, to uproot and to plant, to tear down and to build, to dream and to achieve dreams. But every ambition and every achievement must bow to the lordship and the glory of the Lord Jesus Christ.

So it must be noted that the rescue and redirection of the desire of our hearts concerning what we seek to achieve is a work in progress. I wish I could say that what always motivates me to do what I do and say what I say is a heartfelt ambition for the glory of God and the success of his kingdom, but it is not. I wish that the ways I spend my money and invest my time was always motivated by vertical ambition, but they aren't. I wish I could say that God is always at the center of every ambition of the thoughts of my heart, but he is not. I wish I could say that I always want every achievement in my life to be a finger pointing to God's existence and his glory, but I can't. So it must be said that for me, and I'm sure for you, ambition is a spiritual battleground, and it must also be said that in the leadership community of the church, ambition for God's glory and his kingdom easily and subtly morphs into something else.

WHAT GLORY: AN ACHIEVEMENT STORY

They were young and ambitious. They loved the gospel, and they loved their city. They really did want to achieve great things for God. They didn't just want to be gospel sayers; they wanted to be doers as well. They believed that the transforming grace of Jesus had the power to transform every aspect of people's lives and the communities in which they lived. They were determined to be big-kingdom achievers who God would use to rescue thousands of little-kingdom captives. They weren't proud; they were confident in God's presence, power, and promises. In their gatherings they preached a clear, well-applied gospel message and invited people into God-exalting worship. And they took the gospel to the streets, not only proclaiming grace but doing acts of mercy that directly addressed the particular groaning of their community. They worked hard, planned big, and trusted that God would produce results.

Of course, they revised and revised again their gospel achievement plan, but as they did, they began to see results. It was dribs and drabs at first, but before long people began coming to Christ, and community ministries were noticed and welcomed. Before long they outgrew both their building and their staff. They looked for a much bigger facility to better house what they wanted to achieve and hired people to make sure they accomplished their goals. No one on the inside would have noticed it, but a shift was taking place. Thankfulness to God for what he had done had begun to compete with pride in accomplishment. Less and less time was invested in fellowship and worship during leadership meetings, and more and more time was spent analyzing the stats and strategizing goals. Leaders progressively separated from the body of Christ and became less candid, approachable, and accountable.

Thousands attended across multiple campuses each Sunday, and millions of dollars were collected each year. The leadership community had become a very different culture from the humble, grace-based community they once had been. The elders no longer functioned as the pastors to the pastors or as the spiritual guides and counselors of the congregation. No, they functioned week in and week out like the corporate board of a religious institution. The only thing that distinguished their board meetings from the corporate board down the street was a short devotional and time of prayer before each meeting. The deacons were no longer a mercy ministry board but more like the church's executive accountants and property managers. Growth and money now dominated their discussions and their vision.

Increasingly staff members were afraid of doing anything that would get in the way of corporate achievement. So few pastors and staff had the courage to confess to personal struggle or ministry failure. Staff that didn't achieve or who questioned decisions or values were quickly let go. Much of the staff was discouraged and exhausted, but few would confess it. Burned-out pastors and staff members resigned with little desire to continue in ministry. No one seemed to ask how the church could be the church as described in the New Testament if the leadership no longer functioned as the gospel community that the church was redeemed to be.

None of this happened all at once, and little of it was self-conscious or intentional, but subtle changes had radically altered the culture, mentality, and values of the leadership community. It was all masked by the hungry crowds that still came and the many ministries that continued to grow. The church was no longer just a much bigger rendition of what it had been in its early days; it had progressively become something very different. At the heart level, leaders had changed, and before long, the changed leadership community would, in pride of achievement and unapproachability of spirit, destroy what God had so graciously built. Could it be, in your leadership community, that there are signs that the glory of achievement has begun to replace the glory of God as the most powerful motivator in the hearts of your leaders and of the way leadership plans, assesses, and does its work?

Gospel-oriented achievement is a beautiful thing, but the desire to achieve becomes dangerous when it rises to rule the hearts of the leadership community. Below are signs that indicate when achievement has become dangerous. Use these to evaluate your leadership community and for the purpose of honest leader self-examination.

1. Achievement becomes dangerous when it
dominates the leadership community.

Let me begin by acknowledging that God has ordained us to do ministry where money is a needed concern, where there are necessary business aspects to what we do, where strategic planning is important, and where the numeric growth of the church requires more property, bigger buildings, a greater focus on facility maintenance, and a progressively growing community of employees to staff it all. None of these things are wrong or dangerous; they are necessities of a wise stewardship of a growing ministry. But these things must not become so dominant that they begin to change us and the way that we think about ourselves and the ministry to which we have been called. We cannot allow ourselves to migrate from being pastor and ministry leaders to being the corporate board of a religious enterprise. We cannot allow ourselves to move from being humble, approachable gospel servants to being rather proud and not-so-approachable institutional achievers.

Achievement plans for a local church are not necessarily enemies of humble gospel ministry, but as you experience ministry success and numeric growth, they are difficult to hold in proper balance. When humble, gospel-passionate pastors, preachers, and leaders over time morph into institutionally focused administrators or vision casters, they tend to lose some of their gospel passion, and the church or ministry suffers as a result. Yes, we should be ambitious for the expansion of God's kingdom of glory and grace, but we must also recognize that as long as sin still resides in our hearts, achievement is a spiritual war zone that is not only littered with pastor or leader casualties but has reduced many who are still in ministry to the ranks of the walking wounded. Hear the cautions for us in the spiritual history of Israel, as they tasted the success and affluence of the promised land:

> It was I who knew you in the wilderness,
>> in the land of drought;
> but when they had grazed, they became full,
>> they were filled, and their heart was lifted up;
>> therefore they forgot me. (Hos. 13:5–6)

In your ministry community, has the quest for institutional achievement become dominant? Don't answer too quickly.

*2. Achievement becomes dangerous when it
controls our definition of leaders.*

The qualifications for ministry in the church of Jesus Christ are radically different from the way we typically think about the makeup of a true leader. I want to listen to what people in a church or ministry say after announcing that someone has real leadership qualities. I want to hear what they think those qualities are. Should people be ceded position, authority, or leadership in a ministry or church because they have been successful in ministry, because they have the drive to get a job done, because they have handled their finances well, because they are persuasive communicators, or because they have an impressive resume?

Consider, for a moment, the radical nature of the qualities that God says in 1 Timothy 3:2–7 make for a long-term, faithful ministry leader, the kind of leader every influential church or ministry needs:

- Above reproach
- Husband of one wife
- Sober-minded
- Self-controlled
- Respectable
- Hospitable
- Able to teach
- Not a drunkard
- Not violent
- Gentle
- Not quarrelsome
- Not a lover of money
- Managing his household well
- Not a recent convert
- Well thought of by outsiders

I want to make two observations about long-term success in ministry. First, in a general sense, God wants pastors and leaders to be successful because he loves his kingdom and his bride, the church, but in God's estimation, long-term faithfulness that produces fruit in ministry is rooted in humble, godly character. A second thing that this leader-quality list presses in on us is that ultimately God is the achiever; our calling is to be usable tools in his powerful hands. Because we are not sovereign over the situation in which we minister, because we have no power to change people's hearts, because we are often in the way of instead of being part of what God is doing, and because we cannot predict the future, we have no ability on our own to achieve ministry growth or success. We are called to faithfulness of character—character, by the way, that only God can produce in us, and God is sovereign over the miracle of redeeming grace and the expansion of his kingdom. *Where in your leadership community have you become more focused on doing than on being?*

*3. Achievement becomes dangerous when it
forms our view of success and failure.*

I am persuaded that when an achievement focus dominates a leadership community, it tends to have an erroneous definition of failure. Failure is not the inability to produce desired results. There are so many things in ministry in this fallen world, over which we will never have control, that influence outcomes. If hard, disciplined, faithful, well-planned, appropriately executed, and joyful ministry work does not guarantee results, then the lack of desired results should not define leadership failure. Remember Paul's words in 1 Corinthians 3:7: "Neither he who plants nor he who waters is anything, but only *God who gives the growth.*"

True failure is always a character issue. It is rooted in laziness, pride, lack of discipline, self-excusing, failure to plan well, lack of joy in labor, and failure to persevere during hardship. Failure is not first a matter of results; failure is always first a matter of the heart. It's failure when I have not invested my God-given time, energy, and gifts in the work God has called me to do. Ministry laziness and unfaithfulness are failure.

If, however, a leadership community is too result- or achievement-focused, it will tend to disrespect a leader who hasn't achieved desired outcomes even though he has been a faithful steward of the gifts and opportunities God has given him. Rather than reminding themselves once again that they are utterly dependent on God to grow the seeds that they have planted and watered, that leadership community will tend to think that they have put the wrong person in the job, will set that leader aside, and will look for someone else to do the task. I can't tell you how many faithful pastors and leaders I have counseled who have come to think of themselves as failures because their work didn't achieve what they and the community around them hoped it would achieve. In ministry, success and failure are not a matter of results but are defined by faithfulness. Faithfulness is what God asks of us; the rest is entirely up to his sovereignty and the power of his grace. *How does your leadership community define failure, and how does that shape the way a leader is viewed whose work has not produced the desired results?*

4. Achievement becomes dangerous when it silences honest leader communication.

Because of what God has done for us in the person and work of Jesus Christ, our leadership communities have been freed to be the most honest communities on earth. We are free to confess weakness because Jesus is our strength. We are free to confess failure because all of our failures have been covered by his blood. We are freed from taking credit for what only God can produce. We are free to respectfully disagree with one another because we get our identity and security from our Lord and not from one another. We are free to confess wrong attitudes toward and actions against one another because grace allows us to reconcile. We are freed from the allure of power and position because we have been freed from looking horizontally for what can only be found vertically. And we are free, because of Christ's work, to talk about these things and confess how we struggle with them.

But in achievement-dominated leadership communities, that kind of honest talk tends to get silenced. It's not silenced by the plan of any one person but by the values of the leadership community. In achievement-focused leadership communities, leaders tend to be afraid of confessing weakness or admitting failure. They tend to deny both to themselves and hide both from their fellow leaders. It has pained me to talk to leaders who are in regular contact with a leadership community but tell me that they have no one to talk to about their weaknesses or to confess their fear of ministry failure.

It's not that they have been ministering alone, but the functional values of their ministry community make it hard for them to think that they can be honest about their struggles and find understanding and grace.

Think with me about the danger of a ministry leader who feels he can't be real with anyone. None of us is independently strong. All of us drag into our ministry a personal catalog of weaknesses, and we will until we're on the other side. God offers us his enabling grace because we still need it. Denial of weakness is never a pathway to good things. We all fail somehow, someway every day. Often failure is the workroom God uses in our lives to reform us to be what we need to be in order to be more successful tools in his hands. And, by the way, we are commanded in Scripture to confess our faults to one another. I will say more about this in the next chapter.

Hiding, denial, and fear will keep a ministry community from spiritual health, and the lack of spiritual health will prohibit the ministry longevity that is a necessary ingredient in realizing long-term results. *Do your leaders feel free to confess to personal weakness and failure, knowing that when they do, they will be greeted with grace?*

5. Achievement becomes dangerous when it causes leaders to view disciples as consumers.

Here is the danger: in local church ministry it is much, much easier to build church stuff than it is to build people. Building facilities, multiplying ministries, and planning a yearly catalog of events are much more immediately satisfying and fulfilling than the long-term, often frustrating and discouraging work of leadership giving themselves to the gospel work of building a community of disciples of Jesus Christ. So it is tempting to define ministry by the church stuff that we have built, managed, and maintained rather than by the numbers of people who are in the process of having their lives turned inside out and upside down by the progressive work of transforming grace.

Yes, there are facilities that need to be designed and built, there are programs that need to be established and staffed, and there are events that need to be scheduled, but these things must not be viewed as the heart of the ministry work to which we have been called as a leadership community, and they must not dominate our ministry energy, efforts, conversations, and decisions, and they surely must not define the way we assess ministry success.

Our ministry passion and energies should be focused on doing everything we can to lead the people entrusted into our care into a deeper love for and service to Jesus so that everything we do serves this disciple-making purpose. When this central calling is replaced with institution building, potential disciples get turned into consumers. They tend to view the church as a location with a set of facilities and a catalog of events, and they shop for what they think will meet their needs or the needs of their family. The church is not a vital part of their lives, like an organ or a limb of one's physical body. Instead, the church is just an event they attend, stepping out of their lives to do church stuff and then stepping back into their lives when the event is over. A disciple has no such separation in his thinking. For him, being part of the body of Christ is an identity that doesn't just define a set of gatherings he attends but redefines everything in his life. Everything about him—his relationships, his work, his time, his money—is being transformed because he is part of the transformational community of disciples called "the church."

This work is much, much harder and requires much more patience and grace than achieving facility and program goals, and the gospel tells us why. We have the power to build church stuff, but we have no power whatsoever to build people. When it comes to people building, we are completely dependent on transforming grace. The Savior is the people-building achiever who uses us as his tools but works in his own way and on his own time. What are you seeking to build and how will you know that you have achieved your goals? It really is true that ministry achievement becomes dangerous when it turns potential disciples into consumers. *How has the way you have built the church and the way you think about your job as leaders influenced the way your congregation thinks about the church and their relationship to it?*

6. Achievement becomes dangerous when it tempts us to see people as obstacles.

We can't allow ourselves to be so intent on achieving great things for God that we develop negative attitudes toward the messy people of God who are intended to be the objects of the ministry to which we have been called. God knew that if he placed his church in a fallen world that it would be inefficient and a bit chaotic. But the mess of ministry is God's mess, a mess that drives leaders beyond the borders of their own wisdom and strength to rely on the presence, power, and promises of the one who sent them.

I can't resist repeating a story I've written about elsewhere, because it is such an example of this point. I was teaching a pastoral ministry class and telling my students stories of the messy and sometimes difficult people God called me to lead, when a student interrupted and said, "Okay, Professor Tripp, we know that we will have these *projects* in our church; tell us what to do with them so we can get back to the work of ministry." In his view, these people were obstacles in the way of ministry rather than the focus of his ministry. Of course ministry is messy! The church is a community of unfinished people living in a broken world and still in need of God's forgiving and transforming grace. The church isn't meant, for either leaders or those being led, to be comfortable; it's meant to be personally transformational.

It's important as leaders not to lose sight of the fact that we have been called to people who are in need of fundamental heart and life change, while we confess that we, like them, are often in the way of what God is doing rather than being part of it. The church will never be a community of spiritually mature people if leaders are so busy achieving that they fail to treat immature people with patience and grace. Church leadership is a people-building ministry; to function any other way is both unbiblical and dangerous. *Has the way that you have defined ministry negatively impacted the way you view, live with, and lead the unfinished people who are meant to be the recipients of that ministry?*

7. Achievement becomes dangerous when it causes leaders to take credit for what they never could have produced on their own.

In church leadership it may be that achieving goals may be more spiritually dangerous than dealing with obstacles in the way of failure. When a leadership community seems to be on a run of success, with numbers increasing, ministries healthy and multiplying, and people growing, leaders are easily tempted to take credit for what only God, in his presence, power, and grace, could produce. This temptation brings to mind God's warning to the children of Israel as they entered the promised land:

> When the LORD your God brings you into the land that he swore to your fathers, to Abraham, to Isaac, and to Jacob, to give you—with great and good cities that you did not build, and houses full of all good things that you did not fill, and cisterns that you did not dig, and vineyards and olive trees that you did not plant—and when you eat and are full, *then take care lest you forget the LORD*, who brought you out of the land of Egypt, out of the house of slavery. (Deut. 6:10–12)

If you take credit as a leader instead of assigning credit to the one who sent you and who alone produces fruit out of your labors, you will praise less, pray less, and plan more. Leadership communities are in trouble when they assign more power to their planning than to their prayer. When you take credit for what you could not have produced on your own, you assign to yourself wisdom, power, and righteousness that you don't have. Then you begin to assess yourself as capable rather than needy, as strong rather than weak, and as self-sufficient rather than dependent. Your pride in achievement not only makes you a proud leader but also sucks the life out of your personal devotional communion with God and your fellowship with his people. Your devotional life gets kidnapped by preparation and planning, and you are less dependent on and open to the ministry of the body of Christ. Further, because your successes have made you feel worthy and entitled, you are tempted to grant yourself a lifestyle and luxuries that few of the people you have been called to serve will ever be able to have. (Please stop here for a moment and read Amos 6:1–6.)

Way too many leadership communities in the church of Jesus Christ are populated by leaders who, because of ministry success, have become unapproachable and controlling. It is sad when the proclaimers of God's grace have come to feel less than dependent on God's grace as they fulfill their ministry calling. God has used the weakness of my sickness-damaged body to reveal to me that much of what I thought was faith in Christ was not faith at all. It was pride in experience, pride in accomplishment, pride in physical strength and the ability to produce.

This is a temptation that every leadership community faces, particularly when God has granted that community success. There are two things that need to be observed here. First, God doesn't call us to ministry leadership because we are able, but because he is. Second, as leaders we should not fear weakness, because God's grace is sufficient. It's our delusions of strength that we should fear because they will keep us from seeking and celebrating that very same grace.

*8. Achievement is dangerous when it becomes the
principal lens of leader self-evaluation.*

Every human being is constantly doing self-diagnosis. We are always
evaluating how we are doing. And we are always looking to some
kind of standard to help us measure personal achievement. Those
in leadership are no exception. Sometimes they evaluate formally,
but most often they evaluate in ways that are subtle and unspoken.
Leaders constantly revisit their track record, evaluate their present
performance, and calculate their potential. None of this is wrong,
and all of it is part of what it means to be a rational, productive
human being. But achievement as the dominant measure of leadership is dangerously single-focused and imbalanced and gives a false
view of the condition of those in a leadership community.

A life of long-term ministry productivity is always the result of
the condition of the leader's heart. Godly leaders, because of humility of heart combined with a robust faith in the power of God's grace
and the reliability of his promises, are able to weather the storms,
defeats, and disappointments that are the inescapable experience of
every leader's life. Because of their humility they become increasingly
thankful for, open to, and dependent on fellow leaders. And because
of their acknowledgment of their need for God's grace, they don't
take credit for what only God can bring about.

Yes, we should assess whether leaders are doing their jobs with discipline, faithfulness, and joy. And, yes, because we are passionate for
the gospel and the extension of God's kingdom, we should be on the
mark, working to achieve. But we must not esteem doing over being.
Think of the beloved leaders whose ministries imploded; almost never
were these leaders set aside because they failed to achieve. Rather, in
the lives of failed leader after failed leader, the failure was more a matter of character than productivity. *Has leader productivity caused you
to fail to ask questions about the deeper spiritual health of your leaders?*

*9. Achievement becomes dangerous when it tempts
us to replace prayer with planning.*

Perhaps every church leadership community should post James 5:1–18 as a constant reminder and warning. Fruit in ministry is the result not of our wise planning and diligent execution but of the loving operation of God's rescuing and transforming grace. He produces the fruit; we are but tools in his redemptive hands. He calls us to himself, conscripts us for his work, produces commitment in our hearts, gives vision to our minds, empowers us to be faithful and disciplined, brings people under our care, softens their hearts to hear the gospel, produces conviction and faith in their hearts, empowers their obedience, transforms their lives, and calls them into his work.

Of course we should plan, of course we should work to be good stewards of the people and resources God entrusts to us, and of course we should continually evaluate how we are doing, but as we are giving much time and energy to these things, we must not let prayer become a perfunctory habit, attached to the beginning and ending of leadership gatherings. As I stated earlier, prayerlessness in a leadership community is always a result of putting credit where it is not due. Your leadership community is in trouble if your leaders are more excited about a strategic planning meeting than a prayer meeting.

A catalog of ministry achievements should make us even more prayerful, because we want to honor the one who has given success to our work, we want to continue to acknowledge that we cannot do what we've been called to do without enabling grace, and we need protection from the temptations that success brings. How esteemed are times of leadership prayer in your community? How often do you go away for a day or a weekend just to pray together? Have ministry experience and success made your community all the more dependent on the Lord? Do you have extended times of worship together? Do you at times meet for the sole purpose of "counting your blessings"? Does success produce worship of God in your community or self-congratulation? In your leadership community is planning central and prayer peripheral? *Is your leadership community a thankful, humble, and needy praying community?*

We should be hard workers, questing to achieve great things in God's name. We should be leaders with an ever-expanding vision for the spread of the gospel of Jesus Christ. In every way possible we should be seeking God's kingdom and his righteousness. We should make radical plans and take radical gospel action. We should never become achievement satisfied, because there is always more gospel work to do. But we must always remind one another that achievement is a spiritual minefield. Achievement has the power to change us—to change who we think we are and what we think we are capable of doing. Sadly, achievement can turn humble servant leaders into proud, controlling, and unapproachable mini-kings. But there is powerful, right-here, right-now grace for this struggle.

The one who called us goes with us. The one who called us will empower us. The one who called us will convict us. The one who called us will protect us. He opens the eyes of our hearts to dangers we would not see without him, but he does so not as our judge but as our Father and friend. May we approach him with confidence, with cries for help, with confession where we have wandered, and with a commitment to be good soldiers in this battle. And may we remember that he fights for us even when we don't have the sense to fight for ourselves.

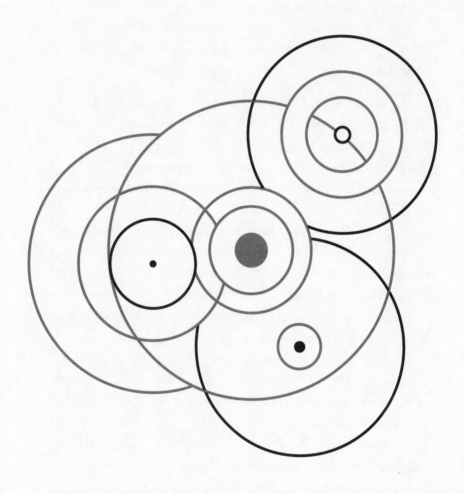

PRINCIPLE 2

*If your leaders are going to be tools of God's grace, they need
to be committed to nurturing that grace in one another's lives.*

GOSPEL

I HAD POURED MY LIFE into this lady. She and her family had oc-
cupied more of my pastoral time and energies than any other family
in our church. I must confess that when I would see her approach at
the end of a service, or when my wife, Luella, would tell me that she
was on the phone, I would say to myself, "What now?" I struggled
with the chaos that was her life and the subtle and not so subtle
demands she made, but I was determined that I would pastor her
through her trouble.

I thought I had been patient and understanding, I thought
I had been caring and faithful, but she had become one of my
biggest detractors. Not only was she highly critical of me; she
freely voiced her criticism to others. It hurt my feelings. It made
me mad. There were times when I wondered if being a pastor
was what I wanted to do. I fought against my anger and resent-
ment, but there were times and days when I lost the battle, and
my focus was interrupted by replaying in my mind what I would
like to say to this woman.

If I had been left to myself, I would have become either hardened and cynical or defeated and looking for a way out. But I was not alone. I was surrounded by an intimate, loving, encouraging, protective gospel community. I was granted the right to be absolutely honest about what I was going through, and I knew that I would be greeted with grace. My blindness was greeted by a community that sought to give me sight, free of condemnation. The community around me was patient and understanding. Fellow leaders took me to breakfast or lunch and lovingly preached the gospel to me. Arms of mercy were wrapped around me and would not let me go. I didn't see it then, but I do now: this community protected me from me in a way that was loving, kind, honest, and encouraging. With all the endless demands of ministry leadership, these leaders took time with me without making me feel like an interruption. This may be an overstatement, but if it is, it's not by much: without the ministry of that leadership community, I might not be in ministry today.

I am sure that my experience resonates with many of you. If you have served long in local church leadership, you have collected your own stories. You've been blindsided by criticism. People you've invested in have turned their backs on you. You've had your qualifications questioned. You've watched dear friends leave your church. You've been through seasons of feeling alone and misunderstood. There have been seasons when you fantasized about doing something else or at least doing what you do somewhere else. There have been times when you've been afraid to confess how hurt and angry you actually are. You've hungered for encouragement. You've longed for someone to come alongside you to help you deal with your struggle without leaving you feeling judged. You haven't always been a happy, contented leader. You too have stories to tell.

CHURCH LEADERSHIP IS HARD

If you have given yourself to building people, you have accepted the call to suffer for the sake of the gospel. Leadership in the church is not comfortable and predictable. It's not a safe place to look for your identity and inner security. Not only is the church filled with unfinished people with sin still resident inside them in the midst of ongoing spiritual war; your leadership community is filled with the same. No one in your leadership community is free of sin. No one is fully spiritually mature in every way. Everyone in your leadership community needs everything the church is intended to provide. So your leadership is internally and externally messy. This is God's choice. He knows your church or ministry is situated in a world that is terribly broken by sin. He knows that everyone to whom you minister is a person in process. He knows that this will make what you have been called to do difficult. But it has to be said that the hardship, messiness, and unpredictability of ministry is his work-room of grace.

Today there will be pastors and leaders who lose their heart and their way in the middle of the hardships of ministry, and many of them will lose their way because they are not warned, encouraged, confronted, supported, and loved by a group of leaders who function as a community of grace. You see, difficult things in ministry are meant by God to be redemptive things. What often beats us down is meant by the Savior to be a tool to build us up. What would make us want to quit is meant by him to strengthen us for the battles to come. Institutional achievement is not the Redeemer's ultimate goal but a means to a greater, more glorious goal: the rescue and transformation of his people. So your core leadership community must be a pastoral community where leaders are carefully and intentionally pastored and where strategies to pastor the pastors are held in as high a regard as missional strategies.

Healthy ministry communities, which leave a legacy of long-term gospel productivity, have longevity and fruit because they are, at their core, communities of grace. Rather than achievement forming how the leadership community forms itself and operates, the gospel does. It's the gospel that tells us who leaders are, what leaders need, how leaders should relate to one another, how the leadership community should function, what its values should be, how it will deal with disappointment and failure, and how it will identify and nurture future leaders. We should look not first at the corporate world for our formative values and ways of operating, but to the right-here, right-now truths, identities, and wisdom principles of the gospel of Jesus Christ. There should be no more powerful influence on leadership formation, mission, community, and methodology than the gospel of God's grace. The gospel is profoundly more than the grace of past rescue and future hope. It is both of these and much more. The gospel provides a lens for us to look at and understand everything that we deal with in church and ministry leadership while also providing guidance as to how we should do everything we are called to as leaders in Christ's church. If we are called to gospel mission, we must, as leaders, be a gospel-drenched, gospel-functioning community. Let me suggest in some detail what that looks like.

A LEADERSHIP COMMUNITY FORMED BY THE GOSPEL

A Gospel Community Is Nurturing

No leader, no matter how successful or prominent, is free from the need to be nurtured. I can't think of a passage that better captures why leaders need nurture, what needs to be nurtured in us, and how that nurture takes place than Hebrews 10:19–25. Let me say first that building and nurturing a spiritually healthy leadership community is like planting a garden. For a plant to flourish, it must be planted in nutrient soil; it must be watered regularly and weeded constantly, or it will not have what it needs to grow, bloom, and produce fruit. So it is with every church or ministry leader. Every leader needs to have his heart, life, and ministry firmly planted in the right-now nutrients of the gospel of Jesus Christ, so that he gets his identity, meaning and purpose, inner peace, and sense of calling from the gospel. Even though he is a leader, just like the garden plant that looks healthy but continues to need to be watered, so every leader, no matter how influential and spiritually mature, needs ongoing spiritual care from the community of leaders that surround him. And every leader still has weeds in his life that need to be pulled out. That weeding work, for all of us, is a community project. Now, to this wonderfully helpful passage:

> Therefore, brothers, since we have confidence to enter the holy places by the blood of Jesus, by the new and living way that he opened for us through the curtain, that is, through his flesh, and since we have a great priest over the house of God, let us draw near with a true heart in full assurance of faith, with our hearts sprinkled clean from an evil conscience and our bodies washed with pure water. Let us hold fast the confession of our hope without wavering, for he who promised is faithful. And let us consider how to stir up one another to love and good works, not neglecting to meet together, as is the habit of some, but encouraging one another, and all the more as you see the Day drawing near. (Heb. 10:19–25)

With this passage, it's helpful to start with the last chapter first. What does a spiritually healthy and productive leadership community look like? First, it is populated by people who, no matter what they are facing, have an unwavering confidence in the presence, power, and promises of the one who sent them. So they do their work with confidence and courage, not because of the pride of success or confidence in their gifts, but because their work is ignited, animated, and shaped by the truths that they confess.

Because ministry is spiritual war, they work to do anything they can to stir up in one another a life of vertical and horizontal love and a commitment to expend their time, energy, and resources to do the good work that God has called them to. So this means their gatherings are not just for the purpose of financial, missional, and strategic planning but to nurture gospel confidence and commitment in one another.

Now for the top of the passage. At the center of the nurturing work of a spiritually healthy and productive leadership community is not a plan, but a person, Jesus. He is our confidence, our hope, our direction, our guide, our protector, and the ultimate nurturer of those he has called to lead his church. He did what we could never do for ourselves: open up access to intimate communion with God.

Now, what I am about to say here is very important. As leaders, we don't just work to develop cooperation with and confidence in one another along with functional unity, but we work to draw one another ever nearer to the Savior. We are doing more as a leadership community than nurturing healthy ministry relationships that result in missional cooperation and productivity; we are also nurturing in one another a deeper devotion to the Savior. The most powerful protection from the dangers that every leader faces is not his relationship to his fellow leaders but a heart that is ruled by deeply rooted love for Jesus.

It is love for Jesus that has the power to crush leader pride. It is love for Jesus that ignites and protects our love for one another. It is love for Jesus that turns ministry achievement from a cause for self-glory into a reason to worship. It is love for Jesus that protects a leader from both fear of man and fear of failure. It is this love that we must never stop nurturing in one another, and if we are going to do that, it has to have prominence and priority in the choices we make in our life and work together. *Would your leaders say that yours is a community that has nurtured their growth in grace and therefore their gospel productivity?*

A Gospel Community Is Honest

We need to take notice in the letter James writes to the dispersed church, that after he gives a lengthy dose of gritty street-level, right-here, right-now practical Christianity, his crescendo comments include this:

> The prayer of faith will save the one who is sick, and the Lord will raise him up. And if he has committed sins, he will be forgiven. Therefore, confess your sins to one another and pray for one another, that you may be healed. (James 5:15–16)

Does the thought of leaders regularly confessing their faults to one another, so that they may receive the rescue of the powerful prayers of their fellow leaders, sound radical or impractical to you? It is this kind of rescuing and protective candor that only the gospel of Jesus Christ makes possible. A church or ministry leadership community simply cannot do its work if leaders are silenced because they are afraid of what others will think of them. It cannot do its work if leaders are hiding sin that robs them of the singleness of heart that keeps them focused on both their ongoing need and the sacrificial work to which they've been called. Fear of looking weak and needy will rob us of the help we need for spiritual health.

Here is the reality that should sober every one of us: there is sin in every church and ministry leadership community, because sin still resides in the heart of every leader. So either we are denying our sin to ourselves and hiding it from others, or we are admitting its presence to ourselves and confessing it to others. But if the acceptance and respect of fellow leaders or of the most powerful leader in the room becomes more important to us than honesty within ourselves, before God, and in relation to one another, we give room for sin to germinate, grow, and take control. Communities where leaders fall are often communities in which humble confession is not only not encouraged; it is silenced by a whole range of unspoken fears.

I need to work in a leadership community that is characterized by forgiveness and fervent prayer so that I can confess the weariness, wandering, and unfaithfulness of my heart to those who will take me to where help can be found. There are a whole host of leadership idolatries (position, power, success, acclaim, reward, etc.) for which there needs to be regular confession and intercession.

If we are afraid to confess sin before what should be the most spiritually mature community in the church, we are sadly living in a state of functional gospel amnesia, no matter how robust our theological grasp of the gospel is. The gospel of God's grace is a welcome to personal and community candor, because we know that nothing can be known, revealed, exposed, or confessed about us that hasn't already been covered by the life, sacrifice, and victory of Jesus. There is no dark thing that lives beyond the reach of God's grace. Hiding sin is burdensome. Manufacturing nonanswers to probing questions gets exhausting. Acting as if you're okay when you're not okay will sap you of your vitality.

One of the sure signs of a spiritually healthy leadership community is the degree to which heartfelt, humble, honest confession is not only possible but a regular ingredient of the life and work of that community. *Do the members of your community fear being honest about their sin, weaknesses, and failures, and, if so, what changes do you need to make?*

A Gospel Community Is Humble

The great apostle Paul, a man with an unbridled courage of faith and a passionate heart for gospel mission, was also an example of leader humility.

Perhaps one of the most dangerous, yet seductive, temptations to pride in leaders is the desire to appear to fellow leaders and those they lead as being more righteous than they actually are. A devastating spiritual transaction can take place in the heart of a leader, often subconsciously. Living and ministering for the glory of God increasingly gets replaced by self-glory. Who they project themselves to be becomes more formative in ministry than who they actually are before God. Self-aggrandizement, like the drip, drip of water that reshapes a rock, begins to reshape their hearts. Humility gets replaced by pride in position, acclaim, and success. The esteem and applause of others becomes too valuable. Pride causes boasting to replace confession, and shows of strength replace requests for help. The long-term health and gospel productivity of a church or ministry leadership community are directly related to the humility of the members of that community.

Humility is a fruit of the rule of the gospel in your life. The gospel will humble you because it requires you to confess that the greatest dangers in your life live inside you and not outside you. The gospel calls you to run to God for rescue because your greatest problem is you. The gospel tells you that no matter how long you have known the Lord or no matter how successful you have been in his work, you need his grace right now as much as you did the first moment you believed. The gospel doesn't work to make you independent and self-reliant, but willingly dependent on God and the community of grace he has placed around you.

I love the example of gospel humility in the life of the apostle Paul. He clearly would not have uttered the following words if he'd been motivated by protecting his reputation and prominence in the eyes of others:

> We do not want you to be unaware, brothers, of the affliction we experienced in Asia. For we were so utterly burdened beyond our strength that we despaired of life itself. Indeed, we felt that we had received the sentence of death. But that was to make us rely not on ourselves but on God who raises the dead. He delivered us from such a deadly peril, and he will deliver us. On him we have set our hope that he will deliver us again. You also must help us by prayer, so that many will give thanks on our behalf for the blessing granted us through the prayers of many. (2 Cor. 1:8–11)

Consider that these are the words of a great man of faith, with his gifts and theological understanding, a man numbered among the apostles. You would think that he had a heart so filled with the courage of the gospel and confidence in God that he never experienced a moment of doubt or panic. But hear his humble words. Not only is he confessing to fear and despair but to the temptation to be self-reliant. He is confessing the need for God to show him again that his hope cannot be in himself but in God and, further, that he is still in need of the help of the prayer of others. In this way, Paul is not a painting we look at and wish we could be like; rather, he is a window to the awesome rescuing grace of the Redeemer. Leader pride produces personality cults, while leader humility stimulates worship of God.

A gospel-rooted leadership community is marked by humility, and that humility engenders a confidence in people that runs deeper than a trust in leaders. It engenders in people a confidence in the presence and grace of the Redeemer and a desire to live in a way that gives all glory to him. *Is your leadership community known for its humility?*

A Gospel Community Is Patient

As a leader in ministry I am confronted and encouraged by James's call to patience in ministry:

> Be patient, therefore, brothers, until the coming of the Lord. See how the farmer waits for the precious fruit of the earth, being patient about it, until it receives the early and the late rains. You also, be patient. Establish your hearts, for the coming of the Lord is at hand. Do not grumble against one another, brothers, so that you may not be judged; behold, the Judge is standing at the door. As an example of suffering and patience, brothers, take the prophets who spoke in the name of the Lord. Behold, we consider those blessed who remained steadfast. You have heard of the steadfastness of Job, and you have seen the purpose of the Lord, how the Lord is compassionate and merciful. (James 5:7–11)

It is to my grief that I have to confess that I am not a naturally patient man. I am naturally project- and goal-oriented. It's hard for me to wait, and I am easily irritated as I wait. It's easy to think negatively about the people, places, and circumstances that have made me wait. The fact that, at this point in my ministry life, I am more willing to wait is itself an argument for the existence and power of God's transforming grace.

It is vital for every leader to recognize that the call to patience is a significant and inescapable aspect of the call to ministry. Impatience in a leadership community will again and again put that community in the way of, rather than being part of, what God is doing in their lives and in the lives of those they have been called to lead. As leaders, we are called to wait because we live in a fallen world where things just don't function in the way God intended. The brokenness of the world surely interrupts the best of our plans. We are called to wait because we lead imperfect people who don't always listen well, think well, choose well, or follow well. We are required to be patient because we are not sovereign.

In order to achieve our ministry goals, many things over which we have no control need to fall into place. To add to this, we do not control when the winds of the Spirit work conviction, commitment, unity, and cooperation in the hearts of the people we are leading into service. And we are called to wait because waiting is one of God's most regular tools of maturing grace. From the perspective of the gospel, waiting is never just about getting what you've been waiting for but, more importantly, about the good changes in you that God produces through the wait. Willingness to wait with patient hearts is a clear sign that your leadership community has been and is being shaped by the gospel.

Pride of accomplishment, identity of success, and the idolatry of power are the soil in which impatience grows, and that impatience always results in a harvest of bad fruit, both in leaders and in those they lead. Impatience tempts them to try to control things they have no power to control, to create change they cannot create, and to move what they have no ability to move. Nothing good results when a leader assigns power to himself that he doesn't have. Leaders who are unwilling to wait value planning, schedule, and goals more than people. This causes them to think of and treat people as obstacles in the way of their leadership rather than as those who are to be served by it. So they don't steward people's gifts well, giving time and room for expression, and they don't give time for God to work insight and willingness into people's hearts. All this creates a ministry culture of fear, where people feel more constrained and driven than commissioned and shepherded. People tend to fear getting in the way of this fast-moving ministry train more than they fear being left behind by it.

But when the gospel is nurtured in the hearts of leaders, they lead with a robust rest in God's sovereignty; his wisdom; his convicting, convincing, and transforming grace; his love for his own church; his faithfulness to his promises; his willingness to intervene; and his timing, which is always right. *How has impatience interfered with the ministry work God has called your leadership community to do?*

A Gospel Community Is Forgiving

I can think of a no more important passage for a leadership than the gospel-lifestyle call of Paul in Ephesians 4:29–32. Your ministry community is populated by people who still struggle with sin and are still growing in grace, so sin, weakness, and failure will challenge your unity and interfere with your work. In ministry leadership, it is impossible not to be dealing with sin and failure in some way. Somehow, someway, every leader you work with will disappoint you. There have been times when my words and actions have disappointed my ministry team. When this happens to you, you will deal with the sin, weakness, and failure of others either with forgiveness and restorative wisdom or with subtle denial, quiet bitterness, active or slow-burn anger, or the disloyalty of slander. The various pathways for dealing with failure are practically laid out for us in Ephesians 4:

> Therefore, having put away falsehood, let each one of you speak the truth with his neighbor, for we are members one of another. Be angry and do not sin; do not let the sun go down on your anger, and give no opportunity to the devil. . . . Let no corrupting talk come out of your mouths, but only such as is good for building up, as fits the occasion, that it may give grace to those who hear. And do not grieve the Holy Spirit of God, by whom you were sealed for the day of redemption. Let all bitterness and wrath and anger and clamor and slander be put away from you, along with all malice. Be kind to one another, tenderhearted, forgiving one another, as God in Christ forgave you. (Eph. 4:25–27, 29–32)

It needs to be said that forgiveness is not to be confused with permissiveness, where you turn your head away from wrong and let it slide. When a leader responds that way, he doesn't do so because he loves the one who wronged him but because he loves himself and doesn't want to go through the hassle of tense and awkward moments that might result if he lovingly speaks truth into that wrong.

Paul begins this wonderful call to forgiveness with a call to speak the truth, and he later describes what that truth telling should look like. It is shaped by a desire to build up in a way that is appropriate to the moment by seeking to root the offending leader once again in the glory and grace that is his or hers as a child of God. Any other way of speaking in a time of failure is unwholesome in God's eyes, unhelpful to the offending leader, and disruptive to the unity of that leadership community.

This means we need to cry out to God for help with our anger, with our tendency to hold onto an offense too long, giving bitterness room to grow and our tendency to give in to the temptation to speak unlovingly to others in the leadership community about the offending person. I will admit, and would encourage you to as well, that tenderheartedness is not natural for me, that I need a deeper commitment to kindness and a willingness to be quicker to forgive.

But I have learned that the more I am bathing my heart in the wonder of God's forgiveness of me, the more willing I am to forgive others. Here's what every leader needs to face. If we are going to live and minister together in spiritually healthy leadership communities, we need to fervently pray that God will rescue us from us, rescue us from the pride that causes us to be more focused on the failure of others than our own, rescue us from our tendency to speak in unwholesome ways when we are disappointed, rescue us from the temptation to replay a failure over and over again in our minds, and rescue us from responding too quickly with the judgment of anger so that we can respond with tender, forgiving grace.

As I look back now at over forty years of ministry leadership, I do so with delight at how God has grown me and used me but also with twinges of grief. I know I have been forgiven, but there are moments and conversations I wish I could remove from people's minds and ears. Throughout the years, my harvest has not always been a good gospel harvest, but often the fruit of my failure to extend to fellow leaders the very same grace that has been lavished on me.

I am writing this because I am sure I am not alone. There are too many angry leaders in the church of Jesus Christ. There is too much gossip in our leadership ranks. Too many of us are quicker to judge than we are to forgive. Along the way in ministry, too many of us have lost our tender hearts. Too many of us are quick to separate from people who have failed us in some way. Too many of us find it difficult to give room for God to grow a young, immature leader. Too many of us are quick to forgive in ourselves what we struggle to forgive in others. Forgiveness serves, anger dominates and controls; it's not hard to discern which of these is the way of the gospel.

Our leadership communities really do need an outpouring of God's forgiving, rescuing, transforming, and delivering grace. All we need to do is scan Twitter to see how quickly we judge one another harshly and speak of one another unkindly. These responses never defend the gospel but rather corrupt its message and obstruct its fruitfulness. But I am not discouraged, because I believe in the rescuing and restoring power of God's grace. I have seen its fruit in my own heart and in the hearts of others. May we pray for fresh waves of that grace across our leadership communities! *Is forgiveness producing the good fruit of personal growth and relational unity in your leadership community?*

A Gospel Community Is Encouraging

I am so personally moved by Paul's desire to encourage and so grieved
that it is not more of a formative value in our church and ministry
leadership communities:

> We always thank God, the Father of our Lord Jesus Christ, when
> we pray for you, since we heard of your faith in Christ Jesus and
> of the love that you have for all the saints, because of the hope
> laid up for you in heaven. Of this you have heard before in the
> word of the truth, the gospel, which has come to you, as indeed
> in the whole world it is bearing fruit and increasing—as it also
> does among you, since the day you heard it and understood the
> grace of God in truth, just as you learned it from Epaphras our
> beloved fellow servant. He is a faithful minister of Christ on
> your behalf and has made known to us your love in the Spirit.
>
> And so, from the day we heard, we have not ceased to pray
> for you, asking that you may be filled with the knowledge of
> his will in all spiritual wisdom and understanding, so as to walk
> in a manner worthy of the Lord, fully pleasing to him: bear-
> ing fruit in every good work and increasing in the knowledge
> of God; being strengthened with all power, according to his
> glorious might, for all endurance and patience with joy; giv-
> ing thanks to the Father, who has qualified you to share in the
> inheritance of the saints in light. He has delivered us from the
> domain of darkness and transferred us to the kingdom of his
> beloved Son, in whom we have redemption, the forgiveness of
> sins. (Col. 1:3–14)

There is not much that I need to add to this beautiful passage
about the character and content of gospel encouragement. I would
only add that since ministry is spiritual warfare, fought on the turf
of the heart of every leader, and since that war is fought in the context of a terribly broken world that not only doesn't function as

God intended but also regularly throws temptation in our path, ministry leadership is marked by struggle and disappointment. So there is never a time in a leadership community—no matter who is in the community or where they do their work, what agenda they have committed to, and who they have been called to lead—when encouragement isn't needed. Encouragement focuses leaders on the glory of what God has already done and on his power to do even more, and in so doing, builds hope, courage, and confidence in the face of whatever difficulties, challenges, or obstacles may be in their leadership pathway. Encouragement captures the hearts of leaders with the gospel and guards their hearts from discouragement and feelings of inability. Gospel encouragement is also a defense against the ever-present danger of the pride in accomplishment, because it puts credit where credit is due, that is, at the feet of the Savior. *Are your leaders more apt to encourage than to criticize and to judge?*

A Gospel Community Is Protective

Being a protective community means understanding that personal spiritual insight, which protects leaders from spiritual seduction, deceit, and danger, is the result of community. Every leader needs protection in order to lead long and well. Pay attention to how the writer of Hebrews paints that kind of community:

> Take care, brothers, lest there be in any of you an evil, unbelieving heart, leading you to fall away from the living God. But exhort one another every day, as long as it is called "today," that none of you may be hardened by the deceitfulness of sin. For we have come to share in Christ, if indeed we hold our original confidence firm to the end. (Heb. 3:12–14)

If sin blinds, and it does, and if sin still remains in us, and it does, then, even as ministry leaders, there are pockets of spiritual blindness in us. So it is vital that we all forsake the thought that no one knows us better than we know ourselves. If there are places where we still suffer from spiritual blindness, then there are inaccuracies in the way we see ourselves and interpret our words and behavior. If, as a leader, you deny the possibility of personal spiritual blindness and trust the accuracy of your self-view, you are not humbly open and approachable to fellow leaders whom God has placed near you to help you see what you won't see on your own.

So we all need a lovingly protective leadership community to help us see things that we need to see but are blind to on our own. If personal spiritual insight is the fruit of God's grace, then a gospel-shaped leadership community functions as an instrument of seeing in the hearts of the members of that community.

I know I need this protection because I tend to be blind to my blindness. It is hard to escape that the writer of Hebrews is calling us to humbly admit that the grace of personal spiritual insight is the product of community. *Does your leadership community function as a protective community, giving one another sight where sight is needed, thereby protecting leaders from the deceitfulness of sin?*

A Gospel Community Is Restorative

Leaders in the church lead on the front lines of spiritual warfare. There will be casualties, and therefore every ministry leadership community must be committed to the work of restoration. I will discuss this much more fully in a later chapter, but for now, consider how James ends his letter:

> My brothers, if anyone among you wanders from the truth and someone brings him back, let him know that whoever brings back a sinner from his wandering will save his soul from death and will cover a multitude of sins. (James 5:19–20)

I am afraid that in the face of the wandering, failure, or fall of a ministry leader, many of our ministry communities are much more conditioned to get rid of such a leader than to work toward his restoration. Restoration should not be confused with being soft on sin. Gospel restoration never minimizes sin. Gospel restoration never values efficiency over character. Gospel restoration never compromises in the face of position and power. Gospel restoration never puts the needs of the institution over the heart of the person. Gospel restoration never compromises God's ordained qualifications for ministry leadership.

But a leadership community that has been tenderized by the gospel, so that its members are humbly aware of their own susceptibilities and the extent to which they are being forgiven and protected, is not quick to judge and separate but joyfully gives and does whatever necessary to rescue and restore this loved one who has given way to sin. I will address this more fully in chapter 10. *Does your leadership community have a track record of leader restoration?*

If we, as leaders, are ever going to lead those entrusted to our care to give their time, energy, and resources to the cause of the gospel in their generation and at their location, we must function as a gospel community so that we have the humility to battle together, the courage to do great things, and the insight to confess and forsake those things that may be in the way. So we remind ourselves of the massive forgiveness we have received and that our Savior battles for us so that the gospel will shape us even when we don't have the sight or the sense to battle ourselves.

PRINCIPLE 3

Recognizing God-ordained limits of gift, time, energy, and
maturity is essential to leading a ministry community well.

— 3. —

LIMITS

IT WAS A HEART-REVEALING moment, more revealing than I wanted it to be. I was a bit embarrassed at the moment of exposure, but it was good for me to face what was in my heart. I was speaking at a large men's conference and was asked that if I could choose a superpower, what would it be. Others had chosen the ability to fly or to be incredibly strong, but I immediately said, "I wish I had the power to create ten days in a week." In so doing, I was once again confronted with the fact that I hate limits. I want more time so I can do more than time allows. I want more strength so I can accomplish more. I want more wisdom so I don't have to invest so much time researching and learning. I want to be infinite and almighty. Yes, it is true; there are still moments in my life when I want to be God.

I wish I could say that I am free of the frustration of the limits God has set for me, but I can't. I wish I could say that I never am tempted to work outside those limits, but I can't. I wish I no longer had to pay the price for denying those limits, but I still do. In ministry it is tempting to try to do more than you can realistically and healthily do. It is tempting to write job descriptions for others that ask more of them than they can responsibly handle. And it is tempting to let a leader work way beyond his limits because his work seems essential to the success of the ministry enterprise.

———

She represented thousands of lonely, frustrated, and discouraged ministry wives who have watched their husbands give themselves to ministry while denying the limits that God had set for them. She had watched her husband progressively wear down and burn out. She had watched ministry rob him of exercise, sleep, healthy community, quiet devotional meditation, and good diet. But most discouraging, she had watched him become an absentee father and a distracted and distant husband. He lived and worked as if he had no limits, and his family paid the price. She tried to talk to him about it, but when she did, he was defensive. His view was that he was doing the Lord's work. He was using the gifts God had given him. He lived with love for the church, zeal for the gospel, and commitment to God's kingdom. His busyness and his zeal blinded his eyes to the danger he was in and that he had placed his marriage and family in. When she tried to talk to him, he would leave the conversations angry, hurt, and discouraged. But on this weekend together, she was determined that they had to talk because she was afraid of what would happen if things continued as they had been. This time she didn't talk about him but rather told him that she was done; she just couldn't live this way any longer. The conclusion for her was this: "It's me or your ministry. I can't do this anymore."

I wish I could say this is the only such story that I've heard, but it isn't. I am afraid that in the excitement, opportunities, and busyness of ministry life, many of our leaders forget, deny, or ignore the fact that they have limits. The only limitless being in the cosmos is its Creator. Everyone and everything has been designed by God with limits, and it never works, never results in anything good, to attempt to live, minister, and lead outside the boundaries of the limits God has set. Identifying those limits and what it means for the way a leadership community makes decisions and does its work is a vital aspect of what that community needs to do to assure that its members remain spiritually, physically, emotionally, and physically healthy. Every leader is a package of God-given gifts and God-assigned limits. It is dangerous to focus on the one without humbly remembering the other.

If you're a leader, you don't know everything, you can't do everything, you aren't completely mature, and you don't have inexhaustible energy. You are not just a package of strengths, gifts, and experiences; you are also a collection of weaknesses and susceptibilities. It is here that the gospel is such a sweet encouragement. We do not have to fear our limits because God doesn't send us out on our own; where he sends us, he goes too. We do not have to curse our weaknesses because our weaknesses are a workroom for his grace. We do not have to hide or deny our places of immaturity because God is able. Our limits and weaknesses are not in the way of what God can do through us, but our denial of limits and our delusions of independent strength are.

So I want to consider with you four areas of limits that God in his Creator wisdom has set for us and how constant recognition and humble admission of these limits help a leadership community assess its plans, assign its work, and evaluate its health.

FOUR LIMITS

1. You Have Limited Gifts

Embedded in Paul's teaching about gifts in the body of Christ is the clear understanding that gifts are limited (see Eph. 4:1–16 and 1 Cor.

12:4–31). Paul's word picture of the human body argues this power-fully. The eye has been specifically designed for sight, and because it has, it has no ability to pick up objects. The design determines the limits. The same is true of every gift that has been given to members of the body of Christ and surely, therefore, is true of every leader gifted by God for ministry in his church.

No leader is designed to know or do everything. No leader is meant to do his work alone. It is dangerous for any leader to be so dominant that the gifts of others don't get expression, leaving that leader to do things he wasn't gifted by God to do. No leader, because he has powerful gifts, should view himself as the smartest person in the room. Smartness is a subset of giftedness. Every leader needs to rely on the contributions of other leaders who are smart in ways that he isn't. Ministry must always be done in humble, respectful, and submissive community because the gifts God has given us come to us with built-in limits. By God's grace I am an influential leader, but I get up every day and do the work that has been assigned to me by people who work with me and are smart in ways that I am not because they bring gifts to our work that I do not have. I would be silly and proud to dominate every discussion and make every deci-sion and assign every task.

Every leader needs to humbly assess not only where he is gifted but also, and as important, where he is not. It is only when I humbly acknowledge the limits of my gifts that I can then surround myself with people who are gifted in ways I am not, smart in ways I will never be, and strong in areas where I am weak.

I am afraid that one of the reasons the ministry leadership com-munity is broken is that we have idolized domineering leaders who fail to recognize the limits of their gifts, who disrespect the God-given gifts of fellow leaders, and who have been allowed to think that they are smart, gifted, and strong in ways that they are not. So they try to do what they were not designed by God to do, they try to manage what they were not designed to manage, and they try individually to do what will only ever be properly done in respectful community with other equally gifted leaders. Pride in one's own giftedness coupled with devaluing the gifts of others is a recipe for leadership disaster. Independent, domineering leadership is functional denial of what the Bible teaches about both the nature of the body of Christ and the gifting of those called by God to lead it.

If God-given gifts have limits, the fruit-producing ministry is always the result of the recognition and employment of a community of gifts operating in cooperation with one another. No gift should be esteemed over another, and no gift should dominate to the exclusion of others. Leaders must push the gifts of others forward, willing to listen and willing to submit to the wisdom of others who are gifted in ways that they are not. Humble leaders surround themselves not with ministry clones but with leaders who have gifts that they do not and are therefore smart in ways they are not and strong in areas they are weak. This kind of community will always produce a quality and longevity of fruit that won't ever be produced by a domineering leader. It is unbiblical for any leader to tell himself that he does not need the full expression of the gifts of others in order for him to do the work that God has gifted him to do.

But there is more to be said about ministry leadership gifts. We have witnessed too many uniquely and powerfully gifted leaders begin to view themselves, because of their gifts, as entitled to a level of power, position, and lifestyle that others are not. It needs to be said that when a wonderful gift is given, the only one entitled is the divine giver. He is entitled to our honor, gratitude, and worship and our commitment to steward that gift well.

Being given a gift tells me about me in that I am not self-sufficient but rather needy and dependent. It tells me I have no ability to do God's work without God's gifts. I can't take credit for my gift precisely because it is a gift. My giftedness doesn't make me worthy of human deference, affirmation, or submission, because my gift doesn't point to me but to the one who has given it to me. My gifting shouldn't make me arrogant and boastful. It shouldn't cause me to think I am deserving. And the gifts I have been given were never designed to function in isolation from the gifts of others. It is sad to see leaders who are influential only because of their gifts take credit for what they could never have done without these gifts, which have been graciously given to them by the hand of God. It's sad to see leaders use their gifts to accumulate power and acclaim and an enriched lifestyle.

Rather than view our gifts as a doorway to entitlement, perhaps we should view our gifts as a call to be willing to suffer. Permit me to explain. Yes, it is a huge honor to be gifted to speak the gospel, to disciple God's children, and to lead his church. But hear the words of James: "Not many of you should become teachers, my brothers, for you know that we who teach will be judged with greater strictness" (James 3:1). Or hear Luke: "Everyone to whom much was given, of him much will be required, and from him to whom they entrusted much, they will demand the more" (Luke 12:48). With ministry leadership gifts comes a weighty burden of responsibility. The size of your expectancy of yourself, the size of your responsibility, and the size of God's righteous judgment are connected to the size of the gifts he has given you.

In reality, when God gives you ministry and leadership gifts, he is calling you to be willing to suffer. Because of your gifts you will suffer a kind and severity of temptation that others don't face. Because of the public nature of your gifts, you will suffer dangerous adulation and harsh criticism. The demands of your ministry life will tempt you to neglect your personal devotional life. The attractiveness of public ministry will tempt you to neglect the private ministry of marriage, family, and friendship. Your gifts will tempt you to be demanding, irritable, and impatient with people of lesser gifts or who happen to be in the way of what you want. You will be tempted to confuse your giftedness with your level of spiritual maturity. Yes, it is true: your gifts mean you have been called to suffer for the sake of the giver and what he intends to do through you (see 2 Cor. 1:3–11).

No one leader is gifted in every way, and every leader suffers because of the gifts he has been given. Recognizing the limits of God-given gifts and the responsibility and suffering that come with those gifts is an essential part of a ministry community establishing and maintaining not only its fruitfulness but also its ongoing spiritual health. *A leadership community that humbly recognizes the limits of God-given gifts will establish a ministry culture of respectful, appreciative, and joyful cooperation.*

2. You Have Limited Time

Time has been set for us; we didn't have a vote, and we have zero ability to escape. The time structure that shapes the existence of all God's creatures bursts off the page of Genesis 1. In one of his first and more significant acts as Creator, God lays down the structure of seven days, along with the structure of Sabbath rest. As a leader, you simply cannot ignore the limits placed on you by this plan and maintain spiritual and relational health and a life of long-term ministry effectiveness. It seems ridiculously obvious to say, but nonetheless important, that you will never get thirty hours in a day, and you will never grab nine days in a week. And you will always need Sabbath rest no matter how mature you become or how many leaders work alongside you.

Every limit that God has set for us has been set because God knows whom he's created; he knows how we were designed to live and in love does not require more of us than we are capable of doing. Limits not only reveal his wisdom; they also express his love. Limits are not a prison; they are a grace. You cannot allow your leadership community to assign more work to a leader than can be done in the time allotted to him or her. You cannot ask a person to pile work upon work, day after day, without periodic Sabbaths of rest. There are few more important things for a spiritually healthy leadership community to consider than the time limits that God designed for his creation from the get-go.

One other observation about the time contraints we live within. These were part of God's perfect plan for people and for a world that had not yet been damaged and complicated by sin. If in a perfect world these were seen as a necessity for sin-free people in an undamaged world, how much more significant are they for us as we now grapple with the exhausting complications, discouragements, brokenness, and temptations of the surrounding world and with our own divided heart and its conflicting motives? Sin causes us to push against God's wise and loving boundaries. Sin causes us to deny our susceptibilities and to assign more power to ourselves than we have. Sin tempts us to think that we know better and that we do not need what God knew we would all need.

But let me make even more practical the importance of a leadership community recognizing and submitting to God-given limits of time. I want to paint a visual in your mind. Picture a triangle of interlocking circles, with one circle at the top point and two interlocking circles forming the bottom of the triangle. So there are three interlocking circles of the same size. Those circles are meant to represent the three vital dimensions of your life. The top circle is your spiritual life (I know that all of life is spiritual), that is, your life of personal worship, devotion, and spiritual discipline. The left bottom circle is your relational life, that is, marriage, parenting, body of Christ, friends, and neighbors. The right bottom circle is your labor life, that is, your life of gospel ministry and church or ministry leadership. These are the three major areas of your life that God has designed to fill your 24/7, along with the Sabbath of leisure and rest.

Above, below, right, and left of this pyramid of interlocking circles of calling and responsibility, you have nothing, because you will never have 29/7 or 24/10.

Now, stay with me here. This means that as one of these areas of your life grows, it can't grow outward, because there is no outward. God chose to give you only twenty-four hours in a day and seven days in a week, and you will never get anything more. So if one of these three circles grows, it will of necessity cause another circle to shrink. This is where a leadership community gets into trouble. When you unwittingly deny God-given limits of time, you assign more ministry work than a leader can do without shrinking the amount of time he can invest in other vital and unavoidable areas of calling and responsibility. How many ministry families have been damaged because ministry work began to take up family time? So more ministry means the leader spends less than the needed time investing in his marriage, parenting his children, fellowshipping with his church family, and serving his neighbors.

As leaders in the body of Christ, we have to quit acting as if balancing family and ministry responsibilities is the inescapable catch-22 of ministry life. God is too wise, loving, patient, and kind to ever do that to us. We have to resist a "try harder, do more" leadership culture that results in unrealistic expectations, achievement idolatry, and a whole basket of bad fruit. I've written and spoken about this before, but I must also mention it here: in the New Testament there is no lengthy or detailed discussion of the tension between ministry and family that we seem to take for granted. This discussion is not there, because the Lord of the church would never call us to one area that would necessitate our neglecting or disobeying another such area. One of the reasons that tension is so often there is that we tend to ignore or deny the wise and loving time limits God has set for us. It really is possible to have a spiritually and relationally healthy family (circle of fellowship and friends) and have a dedicated and productive ministry life at the same time.

The limits of time is yet another argument for ministry always being done in community, so that no single leader attempts or is assigned to do more than he can responsibly do while also giving proper focus to the other things that God has called him to. Are your leaders working too long and too hard? Are their assigned responsibilities setting up tension with other areas of life? Do you have a mechanism for monitoring this? Are your leaders worn out? Have you watched leaders burn out? Have you talked to wives or friends to see how those relationships have been affected? Are your leaders too busy to give adequate time to worshipful devotions, meditative study of Scripture, and a robust life of prayer? Is this concern a regular part of your discussions together as a leadership community? Do you provide Sabbaths of rest for your leaders? How often does the issue of time come up when you gather together? Is ministry and the desire for ministry achievement balanced with a commitment to relational and spiritual health in each of your leaders? As you think about God-ordained limits of time, what changes are needed in your leadership community? *A spiritually healthy leadership community always does its work with God-designed limits of time in view.*

3. You Have Limited Energy

Let me just say it from the start here: none of us is infinite, self-sustaining, self-sufficient, or self-rejuvenating. We all are a package of limited energies coupled with certain weaknesses and held together by divine grace. So a spiritually healthy leadership community that produces long-term ministry fruit is aware that every leader is created by God as a duality. We are not a community of disembodied souls. Everything you are and everything you do is shaped by the fact that you are both spiritual and physical. As I listen to the conversation of the church and ministry leadership community, I hear a lot about spiritual health but little about physical health. By God's plan, you and I have limited energy, and not stewarding our physical selves will seriously sap whatever natural energies we do have.

Physical health must be part of the conversation and the shared responsibility of every member of the leadership community. Just as we care about one another's spiritual health, we should have concern for and care for one another's physical health. This should not be a taboo topic. It should not be viewed as intrusive. Leaders should not be resistant or defensive when this issue is put on the table. It is one of the ways we are called to love and pastor one another. This is where Paul's words in 1 Corinthians 9:24–27 are interesting, in that as part of his gospel calling he keeps his body under control. You may be thinking, *Control to what, for what?* The answer is, control to the Christ of the gospel for the sake of the spread of the gospel. What Paul is saying is that until the Lord returns, we will have colliding passions in our hearts. Perhaps it is my passion for food colliding with my passion to invest my energies in gospel ministry. Perhaps my passion to chill out collides with the fitness I need to get up and do spiritual battle every day.

In order to finish the race and not be disqualified, we all must say no to passions of the body so that we can run the ministry or leadership race we have been called to run. Bringing our body under subjection doesn't begin with diet and exercise, but with searching for and confessing idols of the heart that interfere with the discipline to which we have been called and which grace makes possible. You see, the stewardship of our physical body is not an addition to our gospel ministry calling; it is a significant part of it.

Several years ago I looked at myself and had to admit that not only was I overweight but I was overweight because of acceptable Christian gluttony. Here's how it happened to me (and I know I am not alone). If you gain a half a pound a month, you will not notice it, but that's six pounds a year and thirty pounds in five years. My eating was an acceptable form of idolatry, which did not portray the power of the gospel and robbed me of natural energy. I knew that diets don't work, because you can't starve yourself forever. So I confessed my sin, completely changed my relationship to food, and got serious about exercise. Over several months I lost forty pounds and have maintained that weight now for many years.

As a leader moves through his thirties, forties, and fifties, he can't continue to eat as he once did, and he surely can't follow whatever food passions he has. I know I am stepping on toes here, but I am convinced that widespread church and ministry leadership gluttony is robbing us of both gospel consistency and physical energy. The church is sadly inflicted with lifestyle diseases such as high blood pressure, diabetes, and fatty liver. A ministry leader once told me that his physician told him that if he lost fifty pounds, he would no longer need his diabetes and blood pressure medication.

Regular exercise boosts and builds energy. Perhaps many of us are tired all the time not because of the rigorous demands of ministry but because of the lack of rigorous physical exercise in our normal routine. It is my love for my Savior and his gospel that causes me to eat with discipline. It is my love for the gospel that makes me get up and go to the gym or get on my road bike morning after morning. There are mornings when this is very hard to do, and there are times when I am self-excusing. But, for me, these are not ancillary issues; they get right to the heart of how the gospel empowers me to live and to the heart of the gospel race I have been called to run as a gospel leader.

I know this conversation is hard, but it is one we need to have. I would never judge others because of their weight, but I think we must talk about stewarding physical health in our leadership-community conversations. Because our Lord created both our spiritual and physical selves, because he knows our battle with our passions, and because the gospel permits us to be unafraid of candid conversations, we should be glad that we can put hard topics on the table before a God of glorious love and with the community of love that he has blessed us with. This conversation is not about being legalistic or judgmental but about joyfully living in the freedom of the gospel, which is not only our core message but the daily hope of everyone in our leadership community. *A spiritually healthy leadership community cares not only for the spiritual health of its leaders but for their physical well-being as well.*

4. You Have Limited Maturity

I have written extensively about maturity in *Dangerous Calling*, so I won't say much here, but limited spiritual maturity of every member of the leadership community needs to be the assumption of everyone in that community. What I mean by this is that every leader is a person in the middle of his own sanctification. No matter how long we've been in ministry leadership, no matter how well trained, no matter how theologically mature, we are all still in need of future spiritual development. We all have blind spots. We all have areas of susceptibility to temptation. Each of us has character weaknesses. We are all still in need of the rescuing, convicting, transforming power of the gospel.

So a leadership community must not make assumptions about its leaders that keep them from having gospel concern for one another and candid community conversations. Leadership communities need to commit to pastoring every member of that community. We cannot allow any member to live in spiritual isolation and separation. God has called us not just to the external work of gospel ministry but to leadership "one anothering" as well. I will repeat throughout this book: it is my experience, as I have dealt with fallen or lapsed pastors, that around them was a weak or dysfunctional leadership community that failed, in pastoral love and care, to protect that leader from himself.

Every leader needs to be the object of ongoing discipleship, every leader needs at moments to be confronted, every leader needs the comforts of the gospel, every leader needs help to see what he would not see on his own, and every leader needs to be granted the love and encouragement to deal with the artifacts of the old self that are still within him. If this is so, then we cannot be so busy envisioning, designing, maintaining, evaluating, and reengineering ministry that we have little time to care for the souls of the ones who are leading this gospel work. *A spiritually healthy leadership community participates in the ongoing personal spiritual growth of each one of its members.*

Until we are on the other side, we will live, minister, relate, and live with limits. Those limits are not in the way of what God intends to do through us, because they are all the product of his wise and loving choice. What he calls us to is possible to do inside the limits that God has set and that we will not successfully escape. So it is part of our gospel calling to have those limits before our eyes and in our leadership community conversations. We must resist the temptation to live outside those limits or to make the assumption that we are all dealing with our limits in ways that are humble and wise. God is not afraid to call limited people into gospel leadership, so we should not be afraid, with gospel humility and hope, to put those limits on the table, not just once, but again and again, knowing we will need to retain this commitment until God's work in us is complete.

PRINCIPLE 4

Teaching your leaders to recognize and balance the various callings in their life is a vital contribution to their success.

— 4. —

BALANCE

IT'S SOMETHING WE have to deal with every day, something that makes life exhausting and hard, something we recognize better around us than inside us—the world we live in is sadly and dramatically out of balance. The world as God created it was designed with perfect balance.

What is balance? It is everything in its right place doing what it was meant to do. We cannot even picture such a world, where everything is predictable, and there is nothing to worry about, where life is easier to live, decisions are easier to make, and relationships are easier to maintain and enjoy. That's how it was meant to be by God's design—creation in its proper place doing what it was meant to do, peace reigning from the earth's deepest valleys all the way up to the highest heavens. No brokenness, no dysfunction, and no impending problem around the corner—everything, everywhere and in every place, in balance.

The Bible has a name for the balance: *shalom*. Shalom is everything in its right place, doing what it was meant to do, in the way

God intended it to be done. Shalom was the way it was meant to be, but like a fine crystal goblet now in shards on the floor, shalom has been shattered. The world is out of balance, so much so that Paul says in Romans 8 that the whole world groans. It groans in need of help. It groans in need of repair. It groans in the pain of imbalance. It groans for a redeemer. But it is important to notice that Paul tells us that it's not just the created world that groans; we too groan. Why? Well, we groan because the imbalance that has inflicted our world is not just outside us; that would be difficult enough. No, it is also inside us. We are out of balance.

Our hearts struggle to keep things in their right place, so we don't always think, desire, live, relate, plan, and decide with a proper sense of balance. Certain visions, desires, and created things take on greater weight in our hearts than they were meant to take and throw our lives out of balance. What is important to God isn't always important to us. What God knows is needful for us isn't always needful to us. What God says we should treasure, at street level we don't always treasure. Things gobble up more space in our hearts than they should, and things that should have prominence in our hearts often don't. The brokenness, drama, pain, and sadness in our lives are the result not just of the imbalance around us but also of the imbalance that still exists inside us. Thankfully, by the power of divine, transforming grace we are being progressively brought into greater balance, and we live with the surety that someday balance will be fully restored, inside and around us, and things will be where they were meant to be, doing what they were intended to do. Every leadership community should be periodically discussing these things.

The Bible has another way of talking to us about imbalance. It is a term that, on the surface, seems like a religious descriptor but is actually vocabulary that God has given us for understanding the most fundamental functional struggles of every human being: *idolatry*. Idolatry is not just when a religious god replaces the one true God, and it is not just when your heart is ruled by an evil thing. In its most fundamental everyday form, idolatry is when good things are out of balance in our hearts. Idolatry is when things take on a greater weight in our hearts than God does. Consider the words of Romans 1:23, 25:

> [They] exchanged the glory of the immortal God for images resembling mortal man and birds and animals and creeping things. . . . They exchanged the truth about God for a lie and worshiped and served the creature rather than the Creator, who is blessed forever! Amen.

Paul expands his definition of idolatry from the formal religious dimension to the dimension of the deepest worship, that is, the deepest motivational function of the heart. Idolatry is your heart out of balance. The words here are important. Idolatry is when the glory of God the Creator is exchanged for the glory of the created thing. It is interesting and important to note that the Hebrew word for glory, *kavod*, at its root means or connotes "weight." Think of your heart, as a leader, as an ancient scale with weights on either side. On one side is the Creator weight, and on the other side is the creature weight. In God's design, the Creator weight is meant to be hugely heavier than anything on the creature side. Sadly, sin throws the scale out of balance, causing created things to have more control over your thoughts, desires, choices, words, and actions than God does. This means that as long as sin lives inside you, you will struggle to keep things in your life and ministry in proper balance.

I am convinced, as I examine my own ministry leadership life and have assisted others to do the same with theirs, that our lives get out of balance, not first because of the demands of our job description or the multitude of ministry opportunities that are before us but because of a lack of balance in our hearts. In ministry good things become ruling things. Leaders are tempted to look to ministry to provide for them what it was never intended to provide. Leadership position, power, respect, acclaim, and success begin to take on more weight in our hearts than they should ever take. And because they do, they cause us to make bad choices and to participate in regrettable decisions. In the fear of not getting things we think we need, we work longer, try harder, control more, delegate less, and take more credit. Good godly habits get left behind in our ministry drivenness. Necessary relationships are not properly maintained. Private worship becomes perfunctory, if not abandoned altogether.

Here's the scary reality. In ministry, the way you pursue your idols is by doing ministry. This reality should be in the thoughts and conversations of every ministry leadership community. Take prayer, for example. You would think that prayer is the most purely Godward act in our lives, but even prayer becomes something entirely different when our hearts are out of balance. If in a leadership gathering, you rehearse your prayer before you speak the words, that rehearsal is not driven by your worship of God but by something else entirely. God hears the rehearsal! Such a prayer is not an act of worship but a means of aggrandizing yourself in the minds of those who will hear you pray. You want to appear humble, contrite, worshipful, grateful, and theologically informed, not to God but to the other people who are in the room.

If prayer can serve the purpose of something other than honoring God, seeking his help, and committing to his service, then so can everything else in the life of a ministry leader. Every good thing that takes on more weight than God intended becomes a bad thing, something disruptive and dangerous. It's not wrong to want to be respected by your fellow leaders. In fact, you could argue that you can't do your work as a leadership community without healthy mutual respect. But that respect must not take on more weight in your heart than the honor of God does.

Could it be that the lives of many ministry leaders are out of balance not because they are asked to do too much or deal with too many ministry opportunities but because they have hearts that are out of balance? As long as sin still lives inside us, balance will be an issue for every ministry leader and should be a consideration for every leadership community. You see, if you begin to want things out of ministry and leadership that you shouldn't want, other areas of calling will not receive the attention from you that they need. The more private parts of your life (marriage, family, body of Christ, community, private worship and devotional study, physical health, financial health) will begin to suffer neglect. The negative results of the neglect of those private things on your emotional, spiritual, and physical health will begin to negatively affect your function as a leader. For example, regular tension in your home can cause you to be tense as you enter your leadership day, making you easily irritated and impatient with your fellow leaders. Debt can create worry and anxiety that get dragged in with you as you consider important and weighty things with your fellow leaders.

A spiritually healthy leadership community should be always considering and regularly discussing the question of balance in the lives of its leaders. It should always be lovingly looking to see if there is evidence of imbalance in any of its leaders. It should care about the health of each leader's marriage, each leader's relationship to his or her children, the devotional life of each leader, the physical well-being of fellow leaders, etc. You should care about those things not only because you love each leader but also because they function as key indicators that something is out of balance in the heart and life of one with whom you lead. This side of eternity, it's loving to assume a struggle of heart balance (Creator vs. created) in the members of your leadership community, and because you do, to look for signs of imbalance. A war of desire and motives still goes on in all our hearts and will only cease when our Savior has welcomed us into his final kingdom.

WHAT DOES HEART BALANCE LOOK LIKE
IN THE LIFE OF A LEADER?

Here's the bottom line. The number-one characteristic that every church or ministry should want in each of its leaders, and which should be regularly monitored and encouraged, is a heart in balance. What does a heart in balance look like in the life of a leader? Here is a suggested list. (I will resist the cumbersome "his or her"—both here and throughout the book. All of these apply to both men and women leaders.)

- His leadership is shaped by faith, not fear.
- He leads out of humility and neediness, not pride and self-reliance.
- He is uncomfortable with a disharmony between his public ministry persona and his private conduct.
- He is quick to give grace because he knows how much he needs that same grace.
- She does not love power and position more than she loves God and the people he has called her to serve.
- He stewards the gifts of others rather than use those gifts to gain position and control for himself.
- He is as excited about and committed to the private pastoring of his family as he is to his public leadership work.
- She resists being defensive, and is humble and approachable toward others and quick to confess sin.
- He does not take credit for things he could never produce on his own without the sovereignty and grace of God and in partnership with others.
- He does not use ministry calling and position to build a kingdom of his own.
- She cares more about living and leading in a way that pleases God than about gaining the praise of those around her.

- He argues for what is right but in a way that is gracious, patient, and understanding.
- He does not look for his identity in his role as leader but rests in his identity in Christ.
- She leaves the people around her feeling loved and nurtured, even in places where ministry is hard and the leadership community seems divided.
- He never talks in negative ways outside the leadership community about those he has been called to partner with in ministry.
- His leadership is more pastorally driven than politically driven.
- He finds greater joy in the gospel than in the success of any ministry institution.
- She has such a rest in God's wise and loving control that she does not need to be in control.
- He always deals with diversity in a way that promotes unity.
- He does not despise weakness but fears delusions of independent strength.
- He leads out of a generous heart, more ready to give and to serve than he is to demand and to get.
- His leadership is marked more by love than by power.
- She is sympathetic, understanding, patient, and forgiving.
- He is always committed to reconciliation and restoration, no matter how costly.
- There isn't a constant tension in his life between ministry and family.
- He sees his physical body as an instrument of his calling, and because he does, he gives it proper attention and care.
- He leads out of a heart that has its appetites and desires under control.
- She is not more irritated by the sin, weaknesses, and failures of others than by her own.

- He does not ask of others what he is not willing to do himself.
- He is not jealous of or intimidated by the gifts, experiences, and successes of fellow leaders.
- His public leadership is always connected to and driven by robust personal worship and meditative study.
- She is as committed to sabbaths of rest as to the achievement of goals.
- Personal holiness motivates him more than leadership position or ministry success.
- He does not take advantage of the perks of his leadership for the purpose of personal gain.
- He does not crave power but willingly cedes it to others.
- She is known more for joy than complaint.
- He willingly sits under the instruction of others and weighs others' opinions with humility and grace.
- He leads as a sad celebrant, always mourning the destructive presence of sin, while he celebrates the power of redeeming grace.
- His leadership is more of an extended act of worship than a commitment to career advancement.
- He loves Jesus more than he loves himself.
- She loves the church more than she loves herself.
- He gives up precious things out of love for fellow leaders and those they together have been called to lead.
- His children do not feel ministry has robbed them of their dad.
- He longs for the gospel to transform the deepest reaches of his heart, and he is open to the instruments of gospel transformation that God has placed in his life.
- He leads with the mentality of an ambassador and never with the mentality of a king.
- When he is wrong or has done wrong, he willingly submits to loving confrontation and godly discipline.

- He owns his errors and never defends what should not be defended.
- Her ministry is shaped by the promises of the gospel and not by the "what ifs" of an anxious heart.
- Everything he does in ministry is done for the glory of another.

Now I don't know about you, but this list slays me! It reminds me, once again, that often my heart is out of balance. It preaches to me again and again that not everything I do in my ministry life is the result of submission to the lordship of Jesus Christ, desire for the glory of God, and rest in his presence, promises, power, and grace. There are other lords that war in my heart, that challenge the weight that God alone should have in my thoughts, desires, choices, and actions. It is only when God is in his rightful place in my heart that people and things are in their appropriate place in my thoughts, desires, and actions. Leader, you are like me. This is not something we should think about once as we launch into our ministry or leadership lives. No, this is an ongoing struggle and must regularly be in our leadership-community conversations. We have all watched leaders we have respected and have partnered with in ministry drift into imbalance and do things in the context of their ministry or private life that have left us shocked and saddened. We've seen shocking materialism; abuse of authority; misuse of God's money; love of power and position; the use of gifts, power, and position to seduce and misuse others; the hiding of wrongs; the building of cults of personality; broken marriages; angry children; beaten-down fellow leaders; unwillingness to submit to counsel, confrontation, and loving discipline; using theological insight and biblical literacy to defend what should not be defended; etc.

But perhaps we should not be shocked. The war of balance still rages in our hearts, and if it is not recognized by our leadership communities, and if it does not become part of the evaluative and protective care that we regularly do with one another, I am afraid there will be more casualties to come. This is not about attempting to be the Holy Spirit in the lives of fellow leaders. It is not about cycles of morbid, depressing, and exhausting self-examination. It is not about replacing a spirit of grace with judgment and criticism. It is, however, about humbly admitting that between the "already" and the "not yet," we are unfinished ministry in a broken world. There is temptation all around us, and we still have areas of susceptibility in our hearts. We are still capable of craving what we should not crave. We are still tempted to give way to things we should resist. Even in gospel ministry leadership, we all are capable of being full of ourselves and forgetful of God. There are places where even sin gains ground or where forgiveness is a huge struggle. There are times when we want to resist more than we want our Lord to be pleased. We still have times when momentary fear outweighs our hope in the gospel.

Yet in the face of our struggle, grace frees us from the burden of denying that struggle; grace frees us from the exhausting way of acting as if we're something that we're not and from being afraid to look at places where the weight has shifted, and where, at street level, we are ruled by things that should not rule us. The right-here, right-now presence of God's grace welcomes us to be humbly open, honest with ourselves and others, willing to consider what is hard to admit, ready to confess and forgive, and willing to go through tense and awkward moments in a desire to love, protect, and rescue one another. Grace allows a ministry-leadership community to function as a robust gospel community where candor, nurture, and protective love are the norm.

SIGNS OF A HEART OUT OF BALANCE

If you are concerned for the spiritual health and long-term success of your leadership community, then you will be interested in and looking for signs in the life of a leader that his or her heart might be out of balance. My purpose here is not to exegete each of these signs, since they are all fairly self-explanatory, but rather to offer them to you as an aid to the mutual spiritual care that should be the regular and joyful work of every ministry leadership community. And I will remind you again that we do this out of a robust confidence in the rescuing, forgiving, transforming, enabling, and delivering power of the gospel and out of a heart full of self-sacrificial love for those with whom God has called us to lead. This is not an exhaustive list but a sampling of areas to lovingly look at as you commit to mutual leader care.

- Marriage and family problems
- Workaholism
- Lack of commitment to a regular devotional life
- No regular commitment to sabbaths of rest
- Unhealthy ministry or leadership relationships
- Lack of regular, meaningful connection to the fellowship and mutual ministry of the body of Christ
- Debt
- Unwholesome communication
- Anger
- Discouragement, depression, or burnout
- Physical ill health
- Resistance to loving criticism and spiritual care
- Domineering or controlling manner
- Unreconciled relationships

Yes, the world and everything in it once lived in perfect balance. Everything was where it was meant to be, from the highest heavens to the deepest recesses of the human heart. Sadly, sin shattered the gorgeous balance of shalom, and balance has been a struggle ever since. Jesus, whose heart was balanced in every way, came to live the life that sin made impossible for us to live, to die the death we deserved to die, and to rise as a conquering Savior King, so that balance would be restored in our hearts. His first act of restoration was to restore us to God, because it is only when God has his rightful weight in our hearts that everything else is appropriately weighted. He now works by his Spirit to restore balance to our heart in every way and in all situations. Because that work is incomplete, balance continues to be an issue in the way that a leadership community loves and protects its members. But we press on with confidence and hope because we know not only that our labors will not be in vain but also that our Lord fights for us even when we fail to fight for ourselves and for one another.

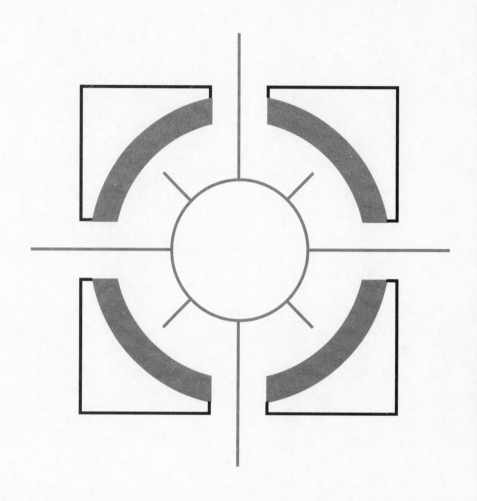

PRINCIPLE 5

A spiritually healthy leadership community acknowledges that character is more important than structure or strategies.

— 5. —

CHARACTER

THE VALUES OF a leadership community shape the way the community thinks about and approaches its work and, more importantly, the way each member views and relates to all the other members. Now what I have written seems quite obvious, but what seems to be obvious is not always obvious in the press of the opportunities, responsibilities, and relationships of ministry leadership. Along the way, in the life and work of a leadership community, a subtle shift in values takes place. I'm not talking here about formal confessional values but about what that community sees as important. This shift in values is subtle, but it fundamentally changes the way leaders do their work. As it occurs, the leadership community experiences a growing discontinuity between its confessional values and its functional values.

This shift happens again and again—what a group of leaders confesses that they value is no longer what they actually value. What they say is most important, they don't treat as most important. What they confess that they want in every leader, they don't actually want in every leader. They are no longer the same community of leaders with the values they once had, but no one seems to know it, and no one is sounding the warning alarms, and no one seems to understand that the leaders' work has taken on a very different character and that the leaders are in danger.

In a real way, this chapter is an extension and a specific application of the previous chapter.

WHAT GOD SAYS IS IMPORTANT

A leadership community is spiritually safe and prepared for a long-term and productive life of ministry only when what is important to God is not just theologically important to them but also functionally important. The life and work of a leadership community is shaped not just by the gifts of its leaders, their vast experience, the force of their public personalities, entrepreneurial skill, or vision and strategic planning, but most importantly by their values. Whatever they value most shapes the way they relate to one another, what they long to accomplish, and what they name as success. So it is important for a ministry leadership community to keep asking the question, "Is what's important to God still important to us?" At the root of many of the heartbreaking leadership failures we have all witnessed is this subtle and progressive shift in values. By the time the church or ministry blows up, the leaders who pilot it are not what they once were, and they do not value what they once did. Most often, this movement occurs in small increments over many years, so small and slow changing that it is hard to notice.

The illustration that follows could be misunderstood, but I think it does picture well how shifts in values subtly take place. These shifts are a lot like how middle-aged men tend to become overweight. I'm not talking about people who have physiological problems they cannot control that result in weight gain. As I said before, if you gain a half of a pound every month, you and the people around you will not notice, but that's six pounds a year, thirty pounds in five years, and sixty pounds in ten years. Then you are a completely different person physically, but not just physically. Along the way you've had to deny the fact that you eat way more than you need, that you have to continually buy bigger-sized clothes, and that you can't walk up a flight of stairs without gasping for breath. You have become comfortable with swindling yourself into believing that you're okay when you're not okay. You make a fat joke when you order the forty-eight-ounce cowboy ribeye steak, but your joke is an indication of something sad, and the people who are with you shouldn't be laughing.

I know some of you will think I'm a stick-in-the-mud, but the overweight middle-aged man I have just described hasn't just had a shift in his belt size; he's had a shift in values, and he is carrying around the empirical evidence of that shift. Sadly, a very similar thing happens to church and ministry leaders. This is why it's important not to assume the permanence of your ministry values or that your leaders won't change. To add to this, because every leader in every ministry still has sin residing in him, the war for the rulership of his heart still rages. Every leader is susceptible. No leader is incapable of being tempted. Every leader at times wants what he shouldn't want, has trouble controlling his emotions, and regrets something he did or said. But there is more.

Every leader of every ministry also does his work in the context of a world where evil is all around, where what God says is ugly will be presented as attractive. And I must add one more element here. Every leader of every ministry works in a world where the enemy lurks, seeking to divert, deceive, and destroy. So it is very important that, as leaders, we are always committed and open to asking values questions of ourselves and to being lovingly confronted when there is reason for a fellow leader to personally ask those questions of us.

I want to look at two places in Scripture that tell us what God thinks is important in the lives and ministry of those he has called to lead his kingdom work on earth. The first is very familiar to anyone who has considered ministry calling:

> The saying is trustworthy: If anyone aspires to the office of overseer, he desires a noble task. Therefore an overseer must be above reproach, the husband of one wife, sober-minded, self-controlled, respectable, hospitable, able to teach, not a drunkard, not violent but gentle, not quarrelsome, not a lover of money. He must manage his own household well, with all dignity keeping his children submissive, for if someone does not know how to manage his own household, how will he care for God's church? He must not be a recent convert, or he may become puffed up with conceit and fall into the condemnation of the devil. Moreover, he must be well thought of by outsiders, so that he may not fall into disgrace, into a snare of the devil. (1 Tim. 3:1–7)

What should strike every leader about this list of leader qualities, the thing that jumps off the page, is that above everything else you could want in a leader, God values character. I must say that I am not sure that we always do. I think there are times when we are more attracted to big personality, powerful communicating, and result-producing leaders than to persons of beautiful character. There's another thing that impresses me here: the list tells us that in God's eyes, character trumps performance. There is only one mention in the entire list of qualities that you could call a "performance gift"—teaching. Everything else in the list is about what moves, motivates, and directs the heart of the leader. Everything else is about what a leader values most in life and in ministry. Leaders who have character, lead with character, model what is truly important, and encourage the same in others.

Do we really look for leaders who are known for their gentleness? Do we esteem leaders who have their vision and emotions under control so that they're not controlling, demanding, or easily irritated? How high is a lifestyle of hospitality on the list of what we value in a leader? Do we consider how a leader has handled his or her money as a valid window into the values of his heart? Are we too tolerant of argumentative, domineering ministry know-it-alls? Do we really value self-sacrificing marital love and tender, compassionate parenting when we consider what is important in a leader? These are all critical values issues. A leader who is quarrelsome values being right and in control more than he values what God says is right in his heart and life. A leader who is not self-controlled can't say no to himself because he values what he wants more than he values what God wants for him. Every character quality on this list is a window into what God values most in the heart and life of those he has called to lead.

So there is never a point when a leadership community should stop asking, "Is there still concrete evidence in our ministry work and our relationships with one another that we value what God says is most important?" We should always be looking for subtle shifts in values that have progressively changed us and the way we do our work.

Here is another question we must always be asking: "Have we closed our eyes to certain character deficiencies in a leader because of the effectiveness of his leadership performance?" Or here is another way of asking this question: "Is there anyone in our leadership community whom we have quit holding accountable because of his ministry effectiveness?"

There is another passage that powerfully captures what God values most in the leaders he gifts and calls to his work. This passage captures what God values in a leader. I must admit that I find this passage one of the most motivating, challenging, convicting, and encouraging reminders in all of Scripture as I contemplate what God calls me to do as his representative. It is a value statement that drops me to my knees in weakness and failure and causes me to cry out for forgiving and enabling grace as I recognize where I fall below its standard again and again. Because of this, it is a passage I visit regularly, and it has become a consistent cry for help to my Lord that has marked my prayer life. Take time, right now, to reflect on the words of Paul in 2 Corinthians 5:16–21:

> From now on, therefore, we regard no one according to the flesh. Even though we once regarded Christ according to the flesh, we regard him thus no longer. Therefore, if anyone is in Christ, he is a new creation. The old has passed away; behold, the new has come. All this is from God, who through Christ reconciled us to himself and gave us the ministry of reconciliation; that is, in Christ God was reconciling the world to himself, not counting their trespasses against them, and entrusting to us the message of reconciliation. Therefore, we are ambassadors for Christ, God making his appeal through us. We implore you on behalf of Christ, be reconciled to God. For our sake he made him to be sin who knew no sin, so that in him we might become the righteousness of God.

In this passage Paul unpacks the redemptive activity that produces the gospel zeal that forms, shapes, motivates, and directs his ministry. He holds before us huge gospel realities that must never take a back seat to what we want for our own ministries, what we want to accomplish as ministry leaders, and what we want from our fellow leaders or from the seductive draw of leadership power and position. We are part of the amazing work of God where he recreates us in Christ, reconciles us to himself, does not hold our sins against us anymore, and then turns and entrusts the message of these glorious realities to us.

As leaders, we must never lose sight of this bomb-drop passage. Here's what it does for all who put their trust in Jesus: it explodes false identities and any remaining pride in personal righteousness. It explodes Satan's lies and accusations against any child of God. It blows away the fear that would make people hide and deny. What has been entrusted to us is beautiful and life changing in every way. No matter your ministry, your leadership position, the daily tasks that have been assigned to you, or the leaders who stand and work with you, it is this gospel that must be in your mind and fill your heart moment by moment as you do your work. The danger in church and ministry leadership is that something else will begin to take the place of the gospel in your mind and heart, and if it does, you will no longer value what your Savior values or conduct yourself in a way that pleases him.

Now, there is a single value-laden word in 2 Corinthians 5:16–21 that is both the summary and crescendo of the passage. Paul says, "Therefore, we are *ambassadors* for Christ." What a picturesque and content-laden word! Think about the only thing an ambassador is commissioned to do wherever he is, whoever he is with, and whatever he is working on. The single call of an ambassador is to represent. Church and ministry leadership is designed by God to be representative in every way that the word *ambassador* connotes. Leaders can't think of themselves first as ambassadors of the church or ministry they lead or as ambassadors of a particular strategic plan or as ambassadors of personal ministry career goals. They must lead with the knowledge that the thing God values most in a leader is that he or she represents him well. In every task, in every relationship, in public or in private, we are called to an ambassadorial mentality, to ambassadorial values, and to ambassadorial functioning.

Now, practically, what does this mean? It means that to the best of my ability, relying on the outpouring of enabling grace, I will commit myself to faithfully represent the *message, methods,* and *character* of the Savior King, who commissioned me. Every message we privately or publicly communicate must be tested by our ambassadorial calling. Every methodology we employ as a leadership community must be evaluated on the basis of our ambassadorial calling. All our attitudes and actions must be measured by our call to faithfully represent the character of the one who sent us. When I think of the message, methods, and character of the King, my mind goes to 1 Peter 2:23: "When he was reviled, he did not revile in return; when he suffered, he did not threaten, but continued entrusting himself to him who judges justly." May we in every way, in every place, in every meeting, in every relationship, no matter how exciting or hard, represent this one well.

Power-hungry leaders have quit being ambassadors. Controlling, bullying leaders are no longer ambassadors. Sexist leaders who do not respect the God-given gifts of women and who may even relate to them inappropriately have forsaken their ambassadorial calling. Esteeming bigness and greatness over humility and godliness means you have functionally walked away from your ambassadorial commission. Using God-given gifts and positions in ways that are selfish, materialistic, or self-aggrandizing is a forsaking of your ambassadorial position. Institutional advancement that compromises the gospel is a forsaking of ambassadorial calling. Leading by manipulation or intimidation is not the lifestyle of an ambassador. Failing to be patient, self-sacrificing, tender, loving, forgiving, humble, serving, gentle, faithful, and kind is a failure to lead as an ambassador of the Savior King who sent you.

I am persuaded that if we made ambassadorial calling our leadership standard, not only would we no longer allow things in our leaders that we have tended to allow, but we would be filled with such remorse at what poor ambassadors we are that we would fall to our knees in confession and seek the rescuing, forgiving, and enabling grace of God and publicly confess our weakness and failure to those God has called us to lead.

It is time for leaders to confess that in many places and in many ways we haven't represented our loving Lord well. It's time for mourning and repenting as we celebrate the grace that gifts us with fresh starts and new beginnings. It's time for us to confess that personal ambition often moves and shapes our leadership more than the gospel does. It's time to confess that as leaders we have given into the temptation to be ambassadors of something other than our Lord. It's time to humbly admit that we cannot serve leadership idols and be ambassadors at the same time. How many times are we going to see the same sad story of the demise of a ministry leader, and the destruction of the leadership community that surrounded him, before we recommit ourselves to God's values and to our ambassadorial calling, and as we recommit, cry out that he would, in love, rescue us from us?

HOW OTHER THINGS BECOME IMPORTANT

Every leadership community needs to recognize that ministry is an intersection of many competing and conflicting motivations. It would be wonderful if every leader in every church and ministry leadership community could say, "My heart is pure and unable to be tempted by any motivations that compete with my allegiance to Christ and his gospel of grace." The problem is that while every leader's heart is being purified by sanctifying grace, it is not yet completely pure and beyond temptation. Vinod Ramashandra, in his book *Gods That Fail,* notes that for the believing community, the most powerful and seductive idols are the ones that are easily Christianized. His words are a pointed warning to everyone in ministry leadership. Here's how we go astray: a ministry leader pursues agendas other than his ambassadorial calling by doing ministry. A leader whose heart has been captured by other things doesn't forsake ministry to pursue those other things; he uses ministry position, power, authority, and trust to get those things. Every leadership community needs to understand that ministry can be the vehicle for pursuing a whole host of idolatries. In this way, ministry leadership is war, and we cannot approach it with the passivity of peacetime assumptions.

Sadly, noble ministry leaders become ignoble ministry leaders, and because their hearts have been kidnapped, they are the ambassadors of false gods (power, fame, material things, control, acclaim, money, or the world's respect), while still doing ministry. In the lifetime of a ministry, leaders change. Sometimes that change is a deeper submission to the lordship of Jesus Christ and to ambassadorial calling, but sometimes it's a drift toward the service of other masters. Everyone reading this book has been witness to the sad drift that can take place in the heart, life, and ministry of a leader.

As I noted earlier, whenever there is a public fall of a well-known leader, my first question is, "Why didn't the surrounding leadership community see it and address it before it got to this horrible place?" I ask because there are a couple of assumptions that seem safe to make. First, you know the leader has changed because if he had been in the early days who he now is, he would never have been called, hired, or appointed to this leadership position. Second, the changes did not occur overnight. They happened in bits and pieces over a period of years. This means that there are not only many evidences of a shift taking place in his life, but a growing body of evidence of a shift in heart sensitivities and heart allegiances. So it seems right to ask again the question I began this paragraph with.

How does a biblically based, gospel-committed, Christ-serving leadership community not move to lovingly confront a leader who has changed, seeking to rescue him from himself and to protect him from false ministry gods? I am going to answer my question in a way that will upset and maybe even anger some of you, but please give me the chance to explain. The reason we are often way too passive in the face of troubling evidence in the attitudes and actions of a leader is that way too often, performance trumps character. I have heard statements like the ones below repeatedly:

> "But he was such a gifted preacher."
> "But look at the numbers of people who have come to Christ."
> "But look how our church has grown."
> "But think about the number of churches we have planted."
> "But we'd never have had this ministry campus apart from him."
> "But look at the gospel resources he has produced."

Few leadership communities say that they have come to value performance over character, but performance becomes the logic behind not dealing with issues of character. Here is the inadequate logic: "Look what this great man has done for God; should we really tarnish his ministry?" So a leadership community accepts what it should not accept, is silent when it should speak, and is passive when it should act. There has been no confessional values change, but at the functional level the leadership community comes to value ministry success more than godly character and ambassadorial allegiance. It's not just that one of their leaders has changed; the entire leadership community has changed, and in many cases, they don't seem to know it.

Let's look at how this shift often takes place. My purpose is not to argue that this is how it always happens but that these steps are typical of the way it tends to happen.

In the beginning of a leader's ministry there is a high level of concern for *character* and a whole lot of loving *encouragement* and *accountability*. In getting to know a leader, he is watched carefully for how he does his work and relates to others. He is surrounded by the kind of community every leader needs. But as the months and years go by and the leader's gifts bear fruit in rich and exciting ways, the leaders around him begin to *close their eyes* and *shut their ears.* Maybe it's anger in a meeting that is not addressed, or an attitude toward an employee that is not confronted, or something inappropriate said about a woman that is not addressed. This powerful and effective leader now has the power to silence needed gospel voices in his leadership community. Fellow leaders become comfortable with *resisting the promptings of the Holy Spirit.* Things are said and done that they know are wrong, and when they happen, there is a check in their spirit, but they fail to respond to the prompting, and they sit in silence.

Before long, rather than confronting wrongs with grace, in their own hearts or in conversation with fellow leaders they are *explaining them away.* As a leadership community they convince themselves that maybe wrong isn't really that wrong. They produce in their own hearts and with one another alternative perspectives and explanations that make wrong look less than wrong. If all this is allowed to happen, it won't be long before this leadership community begins *defending* the leader when charges come from people he has wronged instead of dealing with those wrongs with a commitment to ethical and character purity that is tempered by grace. This once loving, watchful, rescuing, and protective gospel community has morphed into a community of *defenders* and *advocates.* The power and performance of this leader have left him unprotected and unpastored. The success of his ministry is loved by his fellow leaders more than he is. The castle he has built has become more precious than his soul. Fellow leaders have cowered in silence when he has resisted loving concern and confrontation, rather than loving him with the kind of sturdy, unrelenting love that comes when fear of God has defeated fear of man.

No leader can be left to himself. No leader should be permitted to drive away fellow leaders who have godly concerns. No leader should command loyalty in a way that compromises gospel integrity and morality. No leader's ministry fruit should result in his heart not being protected. Every leader, no matter how powerful and successful, should be willing to look at himself in the reliable mirror of the word of God. No leadership community should compromise its integrity to accomplish its vision. No leader should be untouchable by the gospel community that God has lovingly placed around him. Every leader needs confronting and restorative grace.

Ministry is an everyday war of values. But we should not be afraid or discouraged, because we are not alone in this battle. Every ministry leader is the object of God's sanctifying grace. When it comes to the true values of our hearts, sanctification progressively exposes, convicts, reclaims, and restores. Our hope is not that we will always get it right but that God will never forsake his sanctifying work. We may be willing to compromise, but he never will be. We may give way to fear, but he has no fear. We may be swindled into not seeing things clearly and accurately, but his view of us is always perfect. His presence and work in and through us is our hope, and because it is, we can commit ourselves to doing better. We can own our weakness and our failures and accept his invitation to fresh starts and new beginnings.

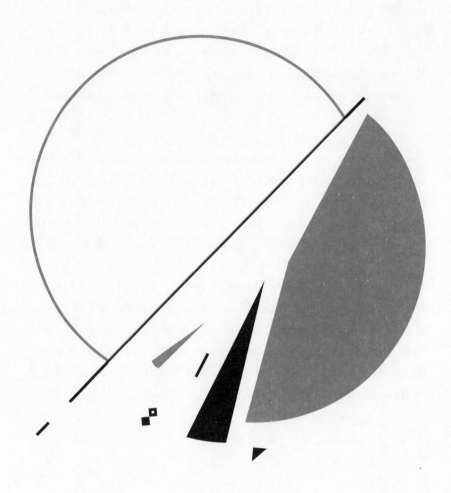

PRINCIPLE 6

It is essential to understand that leadership in
any gospel ministry is spiritual warfare.

— 6. —

WAR

I WAS SO NAÏVE. I thought that as long as I was theologically knowledgeable, biblically literate, and called and positioned by God as a leader in his church, I would be okay. I entered ministry with a peacetime mentality. I had no concept of the temptations I would face. I had little awareness of the attacks that would be made against my character, my gifts, my vision, and my methodologies. I was unprepared for the battle, so at moments I gave way to things I should've resisted. I listened to people I should not have granted influence. I came to the point where I felt discouraged and beaten down, so discouraged at one point that nothing seemed more attractive than leaving the ministry leadership position I had once felt joyfully honored to be called to. Leaders unaware of the spiritual war that is ministry begin to minister with kidnapped hearts, distorted vision, and misguided motivations. They may have changed quite significantly, casualties of spiritual war, but be blind to the degree to which they are different.

Leadership in the church of Jesus Christ is not just a battle for theological faithfulness, gospel purity, and methodological integrity;

it is also always a war for the heart of every leader. Many more leaders fail because they have lost the battle for their heart than because of shifts in their theology or view of the gospel. In fact, it is often the case that theological wandering is but a visible symptom of a heart that has already wandered. I want to think with you about what it looks like for a leadership community to prepare for spiritual war and to do the work that God has called them to do with a wartime mentality.

LIFE BETWEEN THE "ALREADY" AND THE "NOT YET" IS WAR

It is splashed across almost every page of Scripture, and because it is, it is a sobering warning to each one of us. Life, right here, right now, really is a moment-by-moment spiritual war. Scripture handles spiritual warfare differently from the way many of us do. We often speak of it as something unusual, weird, scary, and dramatic. We think of demon-possessed bodies flailing on the floor, people frothing at the mouth—you know, the stuff movies are made of. Now, I don't want to negate the fact that there are dramatic and physical moments of spiritual warfare, but I want to emphasize that the Bible normalizes rather than dramatizes spiritual warfare. Because we live in a fallen world, because there really is an enemy, Satan, because there is evil and temptation around us all the time, and because remaining sin still leaves us susceptible to attack, we live every day in a war zone. Take time to read the passages below that speak in a variety of ways of the presence and normalcy of that war. This is not an exhaustive list of passages on the topic but enough to give you a sense of the sobering warning of Scripture to each of us.

> For we do not wrestle against flesh and blood, but against the rulers, against the authorities, against the cosmic powers over this present darkness, against the spiritual forces of evil in the heavenly places. (Eph. 6:12)

For though we walk in the flesh, we are not waging war according to the flesh. For the weapons of our warfare are not of the flesh but have divine power to destroy strongholds. (2 Cor. 10:3–4)

The night is far gone; the day is at hand. So then let us cast off the works of darkness and put on the armor of light. Let us walk properly as in the daytime, not in orgies and drunkenness, not in sexual immorality and sensuality, not in quarreling and jealousy. But put on the Lord Jesus Christ, and make no provision for the flesh, to gratify its desires. (Rom. 13:12–14)

For the desires of the flesh are against the Spirit, and the desires of the Spirit are against the flesh, for these are opposed to each other, to keep you from doing the things you want to do. (Gal. 5:17)

Beloved, I urge you as sojourners and exiles to abstain from the passions of the flesh, which wage war against your soul. (1 Pet. 2:11)

Simon, Simon, behold, Satan demanded to have you, that he might sift you like wheat, but I have prayed for you that your faith may not fail. And when you have turned again, strengthen your brothers. (Luke 22:31–32)

I see in my members another law waging war against the law of my mind and making me captive to the law of sin that dwells in my members. (Rom. 7:23)

Indeed, all who desire to live a godly life in Christ Jesus will be persecuted. (2 Tim. 3:12)

In your struggle against sin you have not yet resisted to the point of shedding your blood. (Heb. 12:4)

I have said these things to you, that in me you may have peace. In the world you will have tribulation. But take heart; I have overcome the world. (John 16:33)

Only let your manner of life be worthy of the gospel of Christ, so that whether I come and see you or am absent, I may hear of you that you are standing firm in one spirit, with one mind striving side by side for the faith of the gospel, and not frightened in anything by your opponents. This is a clear sign to them of their destruction, but of your salvation, and that from God. For it has been granted to you that for the sake of Christ you should not only believe in him but also suffer for his sake. (Phil. 1:27–29)

Beloved, do not be surprised at the fiery trial when it comes upon you to test you, as though something strange were happening to you. But rejoice insofar as you share Christ's sufferings, that you may also rejoice and be glad when his glory is revealed. (1 Pet. 4:12–13)

Therefore take up the whole armor of God, that you may be able to withstand in the evil day, and having done all, to stand firm. Stand therefore, having fastened on the belt of truth, and having put on the breastplate of righteousness, and, as shoes for your feet, having put on the readiness given by the gospel of peace. (Eph. 6:13–15)

Share in suffering as a good soldier of Christ Jesus. (2 Tim. 2:3)

Exhort one another every day, as long as it is called "today," that none of you may be hardened by the deceitfulness of sin. (Heb. 3:13)

I heard a loud voice in heaven, saying, "Now the salvation and the power and the kingdom of our God and the authority of his Christ have come, for the accuser of our brothers has been thrown down, who accuses them day and night before our God." (Rev. 12:10)

Be watchful, stand firm in the faith, act like men, be strong. (1 Cor. 16:13)

Have I not commanded you? Be strong and courageous. Do not be frightened, and do not be dismayed, for the LORD your God is with you wherever you go. (Josh. 1:9)

Joshua said to them, "Do not be afraid or dismayed; be strong and courageous. For thus the LORD will do to all your enemies against whom you fight." (Josh. 10:25)

Fight the good fight of the faith. Take hold of the eternal life to which you were called and about which you made the good confession in the presence of many witnesses. (1 Tim. 6:12)

Therefore we ourselves boast about you in the churches of God for your steadfastness and faith in all your persecutions and in the afflictions that you are enduring. (2 Thess. 1:4)

Resist him, firm in your faith, knowing that the same kinds of suffering are being experienced by your brotherhood throughout the world. And after you have suffered a little while, the God of all grace, who has called you to his eternal glory in Christ, will himself restore, confirm, strengthen, and establish you. (1 Pet. 5:9–10)

Be sober-minded; be watchful. Your adversary the devil prowls around like a roaring lion, seeking someone to devour. (1 Pet. 5:8)

Brothers, if anyone is caught in any transgression, you who are spiritual should restore him in a spirit of gentleness. Keep watch on yourself, lest you too be tempted. (Gal. 6:1)

[Pray] at all times in the Spirit, with all prayer and supplication. To that end, keep alert with all perseverance, making supplication for all the saints. (Eph. 6:18)

Lead us not into temptation,
    but deliver us from evil. (Matt. 6:13)

Watch and pray that you may not enter into temptation. The spirit indeed is willing, but the flesh is weak. (Matt. 26:41; Mark 14:38)

So Peter was kept in prison, but earnest prayer for him was made to God by the church. (Acts 12:5)

Pray for us . . . that we may be delivered from wicked and evil men. For not all have faith. (2 Thess. 3:1–2)

Finally, be strong in the Lord and in the strength of his might. (Eph. 6:10)

You equipped me with strength for battle;
>   you made those who rise against me sink under me.
>   (2 Sam. 22:40)

God . . . equipped me with strength
>   and made my way blameless.
He made my feet like the feet of a deer
>   and set me secure on the heights.
He trains my hands for war,
>   so that my arms can bend a bow of bronze. (Ps. 18:32–34)

For this reason I bow my knees before the Father, from whom every family in heaven and on earth is named, that according to the riches of his glory he may grant you to be strengthened with power through his Spirit in your inner being. (Eph. 3:14–16)

No soldier gets entangled in civilian pursuits, since his aim is to please the one who enlisted him. (2 Tim. 2:4)

Beloved, although I was very eager to write to you about our common salvation, I found it necessary to write appealing to you to contend for the faith that was once for all delivered to the saints. (Jude 3)

So then let us not sleep, as others do, but let us keep awake and
be sober. (1 Thess. 5:6)

The LORD is my light and my salvation;
  whom shall I fear?
The LORD is the stronghold of my life;
  of whom shall I be afraid?
When evildoers assail me
  to eat up my flesh,
my adversaries and foes,
  it is they who stumble and fall.
Though an army encamp against me,
  my heart shall not fear;
though war arise against me,
  yet I will be confident. (Ps. 27:1–3)

Now, if what these passages portray—that it is true of every
believer and that we live in a daily state of spiritual war and must
therefore live with eyes open, heart engaged, mind alert, and protective gear in place—how much more is it true of those leaders
our Lord has raised up to stand at the forefront of the battle to give
warning and direction? No leadership community should be naïve.
No leadership community should do its work with a comfortable
peacetime mentality. We should be realistic, aware, and alert. We
are not to be depressingly paranoid, because our captain has already
fought the battle and won the ultimate victory on our behalf, and
he is in us, with us, and for us. But we must not forget the environ-
ment in which we do our work and the susceptibility that still lives
inside each one of us.

We're not just leaders, building the household of faith; we are
also soldiers under attack on the battlefield of faith. How many more

casualties of war are we going to lose before we begin to take seriously the war that rages around us and inside us? As God's appointed leaders, we need to strategically plan for evangelism, discipleship, church growth, church planting, and church revitalization, but we must at the same time also strategize together for the inescapable battle that will rage in us and around us as we do this work.

STRATEGIZING FOR BATTLE

How do we strategize together as leadership communities for the battle? Let me suggest three ways.

1. Each leader must humbly accept and be growingly aware of his susceptibilities.

I have seen in my own life and witnessed in the lives of other leaders that spiritual pride leaves you exposed to spiritual attack. No leader is safe thinking he is impervious to attack. A spiritually healthy leadership community is always watchful and alert to the spiritual dangers of life in a fallen world and life as a church or ministry leader. Perhaps there is no better defense against spiritual attack than humility; that is, a sense of constant need for protective and empowering grace that then motivates us to watch for danger and cry out for God's help and the loving help of fellow leaders.

The danger here is that theological knowledge, powerful gifts, ministry experience, and success can distort the way a leader views himself. Until we are on the other side, these things make us susceptible to spiritual attack. The things I have listed here not only don't protect us from attack but may actually be indicators that we are in even greater danger. Of course the enemy wants to damage the church of Jesus Christ and the reputation of the Christ of the church. What better way to do this than to capture and morally wound one of the leaders of the church? Theological arrogance makes us vulnerable to spiritual warfare.

Pride in ministry achievements puts you in battle danger. Lack of openness to the pastoral care and concern of fellow leaders exposes you to danger. Surrounding yourself with leaders who are no longer willing or are too fearful to challenge and confront you is to leave yourself exposed. Failure to cry out again and again that God will not only protect you from the enemy but will protect you from you leaves you exposed to attack. Leaders who forget that they are not just preachers, pastors, and planners but also soldiers in an ongoing war leaves them vulnerable to danger. Any failure in a leader to live in a way that is humble and alert leads that leader nowhere good.

Fellow leaders, we must remember who we are, we must keep mindful of where we live, and we must stay alert to the wiles of the enemy. None of this should be depressingly pessimistic or darkly introspective; it should not be motivationally paralyzing, and it can never be God forgetful. Remember, God's warnings are always loving tools of his protecting grace. Remember too that we have been called to lead by a victorious Savior, who suffered for our victory and who cares more about the health, safety, and success of his church than we ever will. He knows who we are at heart level, he knows the nature of the world we live in, and he knows the kinds of attacks we face, because he faced them.

If your leadership community functions as a gospel community, then your humble confession of personal areas of susceptibility won't be dangerous because it will be greeted with mercy-infused understanding, intercessory prayer, and strategies for help—all fueled by confidence in the presence and grace of the Savior. What is dangerous are naïve assumptions of peacetime safety and proud assessments of personal invulnerability that silence a conversation that every leader needs to have regularly with those in his leadership community. The gospel welcomes us to be honest because it offers divine aid for everything we would need to be honest about. And, finally, we must not let our desire to be respected by fellow leaders keep us from confessing where we are under attack and where we tend to succumb.

2. As a leadership community, personal and corporate spiritual war must be a regular part of our ongoing conversation with one another and a central focus of our prayer together.

I love when ministry communities think carefully and plan strategically for the ministries that God has ordained to occupy his church. I have a deep respect for gospel dissatisfaction, by which I mean that we're not satisfied with a certain level of spiritual growth in the people God has called us to lead, that we keep longing for more people to come into the kingdom, and that we work to see more churches planted. I love when the gospel vision and energy of a leadership community don't wane but grow and grow. I love when new blood comes into a leadership community that has grown a bit passive and respectfully disrupts, producing new insight and new zeal. God calls his people to be on the march, not ever resting, until we hear the words, "Come, for everything is now ready, enter into your final home" (see Luke 14:17). I am thankful for the experts who have studied the history of the church, the lives of leaders who have gone before us, how successful ministries have strategized and planned. I am heartened by leaders who never stop listening, examining, and learning.

But I am very concerned when a leadership community has no time for and gives no place to honest and protective conversations about the spiritual war, inside us and outside us, that is the regular life of every leader in every church and ministry everywhere. We need to talk humbly and honestly; we need to listen carefully and with sympathy; and we need to speak with wisdom, comfort, encouragement, and warning.

There are moments when, because of what we have heard and learned, we need to lovingly stand against a leader whom we have regularly stood with. With the goal of protection, we must stand in his way, refusing to endorse or support something that is either spiritually dangerous or evidence that the enemy has already won a victory in this leader's heart. These conversations and actions are hard; they are most often tense and awkward—the thing of things in most relationships you want to avoid—but you really can't be a leadership community, fueled by gospel love, and avoid them. (For a New Testament example, see Galatians 2.)

We cannot allow ourselves to deny evidence that a leader is under spiritual siege or has been deceived into stepping over God's boundaries because we are afraid of uncomfortable relational moments, questions about our motives, or pushback we may receive. We cannot let ministry busyness excuse the fact that we are not keeping one another alert and safe. Spiritual warfare, if it's as normal as the Bible presents it, must always be on our ministry agenda. The battle is ongoing; we will either recognize it in and around us and respond appropriately as a leadership community, or, whatever our confessional position is with regard to spiritual warfare, we will function as if it does not exist, and in so doing, expose our leadership community to danger. When it comes to the great spiritual war, the victory of our captain welcomes us to be humbly honest and functionally courageous. May we live and lead together with that victory in view.

3. We must examine and defend ourselves against Satan's devices.

It is so important to understand that the primary tool the enemy uses to attack, disable, defeat, and set aside ministry leaders is *ministry*.

Ministry itself is fraught with temptations that play to the complicated loyalties, desires, and motivations of the heart of every leader. Desires for good things morph to become dangerous things because they have become ruling things. Things that are okay to want become things that now control. Along with this is the fact that our sense of identity is always in a state of flux, that is, we are always thinking about who we are and defining and redefining ourselves. Ministry failure can redefine a leader in ways that make him vulnerable to attack. Ministry success can also redefine a leader and expose him to new deceptions and seductions. Public acclaim can alter the way we think about who we are and what we need. Leaders who once led with a servant mentality assess their track record and become comfortable acting entitled and demanding. The trust and respect of fellow leaders tempt us to give way to fear of man, becoming, as a result, less than candid about spiritual attack and our spiritual health.

Ministry leadership is not a fortress against spiritual attack; it's the front line. Theological expertise doesn't shelter you from attack, but the pride of knowledge may be one of the things that makes you susceptible. Powerful gifts don't alleviate your vulnerability, because the deceitfulness of sin can mean that you're better at preaching the gospel to others than to yourself. A strong sense of ministry calling doesn't free you from attack; rather, the feelings of being different, special, and set aside may, in reality, be what the enemy uses to get at your heart, causing you to let down your guard. The desire to achieve, which itself is not wrong, may devolve into leader competitiveness, leader jealousy, and leader disunity, exposing leaders to subtle or not so subtle anger and bitterness. The closeness and intensity of day-by-day ministry may tempt leaders to step over God's protective relational boundaries, making a leader vulnerable to romantic and sexual temptations. Even the handling of ministry funds can tempt a leader to begin to use what has been dedicated for gospel productivity for personal ease and luxury.

The war I have just described takes place in the heart and life of a ministry leader and within a leadership community without any of those leaders moving an inch or abandoning the ministry work that they regularly do. So we do need to study, discuss, and strategize how to protect ourselves from the particular devices that Satan may use to harm the leadership community of which we are a part or to destroy our life and ministry or that of a fellow leader.

Our Savior is alert, possessing every tool necessary for the battle. My prayer is that we would be alert too, ready to use divine tools to defeat what we could never defeat on our own, before the enemy has established a stronghold.

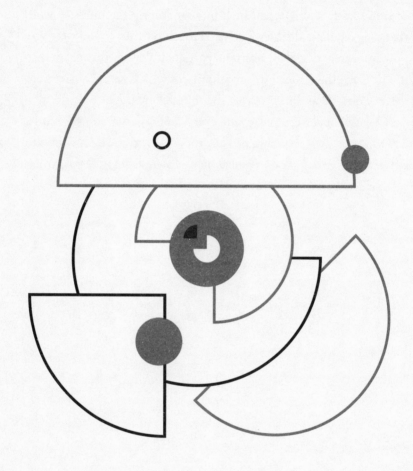

PRINCIPLE 7

*A call to leadership in the church is a call to a life
of willing sacrifice and service.*

— 7. —

SERVANTS

IT'S A BIBLICAL THEME that needs to be studied, taught, and brought to memory again and again because it is so radically counterintuitive. The most often used term for a spiritual leader in Scripture is *servant*. So it is vital that every leadership community does its work, understanding that what God has called each leader to be defines how God has called him to do what he has been called to do. What is the motivational joy in the heart of a true servant? The joy of a true servant is not power; the joy of a true servant is not control; the joy of a true servant is not acclaim; the joy of a true servant is not comfort or ease; and, of course, the joy of a true servant is not position. What gives a servant joy in being a servant is *service*.

Why is service so unnatural for us? Why do we love to be known as servants while not always loving the call to serve? Why do we fall into thinking of opportunities to serve as an interruption, a hassle, or a burden? Why do we count the cost while forgetting the riches we have been given? Why are servant posture and attitude not normal in the hearts and lives of those whom God has called to lead churches and gospel ministries? I think the answer is clear. In 2 Corinthians 5:15 Paul argues that the DNA of sin is selfishness. Sin is self-focused, self-absorbed, self-defensive, and self-aggrandizing—selfish in the purest sense of what that word means. So as long as there are artifacts of sin still resident in our hearts, we will be vulnerable to the temptation to make life about us—what we want, what we think we need, and what makes us content and comfortable. I am convicted as I write. I am required to face the fact that, like every other sinner, my default idol is the idol of self, and because it is, my default craving is for what I find comfortable, enjoyable, and exciting.

So it is an argument for the presence and power of rescuing and forgiving grace when any sinner finds joy in the self-sacrifice and self-denial that are the normal life of a servant. It takes grace to free us from the powerful inertia of sin's individualism. It takes almighty power to free us from the depth of our self-allegiance. And it is all too easy to give way to sin's draw. It is also vital for every leader to remember that the struggle of selfishness is the focus not only of the rescue and forgiveness of our justification, but also of the transforming work of our sanctification. Leader, your Savior has rescued you from you, is rescuing you from you, and will continue to rescue you from you until that rescue is no longer needed. If the leaders around you were to characterize your attitude and actions as a leader, would they say, "He has a servant's heart"?

THE SERVANT STRUGGLE: A CASE STUDY

You don't have to search far in the New Testament to uncover pointed examples of the counterintuitive nature of Christ's call for his chosen leaders to serve. Understanding and finding joy in their servant calling was a huge struggle for the disciples. Let's examine one vignette, in Mark 9:30–36, where this struggle bubbles to the surface:

They went on from there and passed through Galilee. And he did not want anyone to know, for he was teaching his disciples, saying to them, "The Son of Man is going to be delivered into the hands of men, and they will kill him. And when he is killed, after three days he will rise." But they did not understand the saying, and were afraid to ask him.

And they came to Capernaum. And when he was in the house he asked them, "What were you discussing on the way?" But they kept silent, for on the way they had argued with one another about who was the greatest. And he sat down and called the twelve. And he said to them, "If anyone would be first, he must be last of all and servant of all." And he took a child and put him in the midst of them, and taking him in his arms, he said to them, "Whoever receives one such child in my name receives me, and whoever receives me, receives not me but him who sent me."

I've included the context here because the context is very important for understanding the powerful inertia of selfishness. Jesus and his disciples were on their way to Capernaum, and on the journey Jesus spoke more specifically about his impending death than he ever had before. You would think that the disciples were shocked and saddened. You would imagine that their hearts were filled with a combination of grief and compassion. You would expect that in this moment, they did not think about themselves but about their Lord. But the opposite was actually the case. Rather than thinking about the suffering of their Lord, they argued about which one of them was the greatest. It's weird and inappropriate, and the conversation is shockingly insensitive and self-focused, but it is also tragically normal.

As they were walking along the way, Jesus observed the intense discussion, so when they arrived at their destination he asked them what they had been talking about. Suddenly, these very talkative men were strangely silent. They didn't want to confess the subject of their conversation. There wasn't much time between Jesus's talking about his death and the disciples' arguing about who was greatest. Instead of mourning the suffering and death of the great one, they argued that they were great. Instead of being brokenhearted at the thought of Jesus's humiliation, they were focused on their own exaltation.

Now, I write what I am going to write for myself, but also for you. It's so easy for me to divorce myself from these men, to separate myself from this kind of response and deny that this too is my struggle. But the Bible reminds us that these things have been recorded and retained for us because we are just like these people. We are not yet fully free of the inertia that lived in the hearts of disciples and that propelled their argument with one another. This passage was designed as a mirror into which we would look and see ourselves as we actually are.

Jesus's response is at once wise and artful. He essentially says, "Yes, you've been called to be great, but the pathway to greatness is not power and position; the pathway to greatness is servanthood." In so doing, he turned the typical understanding of the power, position, and rights of a leader on its head. Leaders who do not serve aren't actually leaders. They use their power and position and those they have been called to lead to get for themselves what they think they deserve. True leaders don't think that the ministry they have been called to lead and those they have been called to lead belong to them. A true leader knows that people are not the objects of his power and control but the focus of his sacrifice and service. Every ministry leader carries the identity of servant, and any leader who begins to think of himself in a different way is in spiritual danger and has abandoned the true character of his calling.

A while after this in Mark's Gospel, another one takes place in which the disciples respond in a similar way. It's recorded for us in Mark 10:35–45:

James and John, the sons of Zebedee, came up to him and said to him, "Teacher, we want you to do for us whatever we ask of you." And he said to them, "What do you want me to do for you?" And they said to him, "Grant us to sit, one at your right hand and one at your left, in your glory." Jesus said to them, "You do not know what you are asking. Are you able to drink the cup that I drink, or to be baptized with the baptism with which I am baptized?" And they said to him, "We are able." And Jesus said to them, "The cup that I drink you will drink, and with the baptism with which I am baptized, you will be baptized, but to sit at my right hand or at my left is not mine to grant, but it is for those for whom it has been prepared." And when the ten heard it, they began to be indignant at James and John. And Jesus called them to him and said to them, "You know that those who are considered rulers of the Gentiles lord it over them, and their great ones exercise authority over them. But it shall not be so among you. But whoever would be great among you must be your servant, and whoever would be first among you must be slave of all. For even the Son of Man came not to be served but to serve, and to give his life as a ransom for many."

What a provocative conversation with so much for us to unpack. Since the Bible says that we speak from our hearts, it's appropriate to consider the hearts of James and John as they bring their request to Jesus, and of the other disciples as they react to the request. It's important that we don't gloss over the self-focus behind the words of the disciples, but it's also important that we understand that there are still seeds of the same in all of us. James and John come to Jesus and say (my paraphrase), "Jesus, here's what we'd like you to do; we'd like you to exercise your messianic power to give us what we want, and what we want is to sit on either side of you in glory."

On the surface, this request seems way more outrageous than anything we would ask of the Lord, but is it? I must confess there have been times when I have been spiritually discontent because the Lord hasn't exercised his power to make things easier or more comfortable. I'll walk away from a tough meeting, a hard conversation, or an unfair critique and think, "Why does ministry have to be so hard?" In that moment, I'm not just talking to myself; I'm complaining to my Lord. There are times when I am tempted to wish that ministry was more a throne than a cross. There are times when I am tired of sacrifice and suffering, and I wish that God would use a little of his power to make it a little less uncomfortable. Sometimes I don't want to serve; I want to be served, not just by the people around me but also by the one who has called me. In this way, I am very thankful for the way this passage exposes me, and I trust you will be thankful as well.

But Jesus says more. He makes it very clear that we must not take the normal human models as our own. Gentile leaders loved their authority, loved exercising it, and loved reminding people of it. Jesus reminds the disciples that they haven't been called to lordship but to servanthood. They haven't been called to flash around their power and position but to carry around with them the mentality of a slave. Then he uses himself as an example. If anyone had the right to power, position, and authority on earth, it was the Son of Man, but he didn't come to exercise his power in order to be served, but to serve, even to the point of death. We would all do well to have Jesus as a more influential model of leadership than the cultural or corporate models we sometimes look to.

These passages are quite an indictment against entitled, demanding, controlling, power- and positioned-focused ministry leaders! Why do ministry leaders get mad when someone disagrees with them or questions their plans? Why are ministry leaders intimidated by the gifts of other leaders? Why do leaders treat the people around them as if they are there to serve them instead of the other way around? Why do ministry leaders speak disrespectfully to fellow leaders or support staff, at times using language they should not use? Why do ministry leaders avoid tough conversations that need to be had? Why do ministry leaders build off-the-record alliances with other leaders so that their ideas will win the day? Why is unity difficult and division natural? The answer to all these questions is that it's so hard for us to willingly, patiently, joyfully, lovingly, and sacrificially serve. We may not be as bold as James and John, but there's evidence among us that their struggle is our struggle as well.

TO LEAD IS TO SERVE, TO SERVE IS BEING WILLING TO SUFFER

There simply is no such thing as a call to ministry leadership that isn't also a call to a life of servanthood, and there is no such thing as a call to servanthood that isn't also a call to suffer. As I travel around the world, I converse with young ministry leaders, and in these conversations I hear the same themes over and over again. These young leaders tell me about their exhaustion, how demanding ministry is, how much they just need a break or an adjustment in their schedule, and how difficult the people they lead. Several things have come into my mind as I've listened to these conversations. Of course, it is wise to know our limits, to construct a reasonable schedule and to know when it's godly to say no. But there is something going on in the hearts and lives of these leaders and the leadership communities that leaves me concerned.

Before I talk about the nature of my concern, I want to make a pastoral observation. God is sovereign, and he writes your story, and because he does, he is in control of where you have been positioned in ministry and all the things you are tasked with there. Your complaint about schedule is never just about schedule, your complaint about exhaustion is never just about how tired you are, and your complaint that you never seem to get the break you think you need is never just about time. All horizontal complaints have a vertical component. Even though I may not be aware of it, my complaint about the bad service at a restaurant is not just a complaint about my particular server but also about the manager who trained her and watches how she does her work.

Grumbling about horizontal difficulty is at once a complaint against the one who lords over those difficulties. And here's what's deadly about this. A life of quiet or not so quiet complaint hammers away at your confidence in the wisdom, goodness, and faithfulness of God. It causes you to rest less comfortably in his care. Why? Well, because you tend not to seek out and rely on someone whom you no longer trust. A leadership community that has developed a culture of grumbling is, because of that, in spiritual danger. It is simply hard to willingly and joyfully serve the master you don't trust in the way you once did, no matter what your formal theology tells you about his wisdom, goodness, and faithfulness.

Now to my concern. I am convinced that the life and ministry of a leader who is marked by low-grade grumbling, feelings of dissatisfaction, or conscious complaint indicate a foundational misunderstanding of the nature of the church and ministry calling. Church life was not designed to be comfortable. What is the church? It's a chosen gathering of unfinished people, still grappling with the selfishness of sin and the seduction of temptation, living in a fallen world, where there is deception and dysfunction all around. There is nothing comfortable or easy in this plan. The church is intended to be messy and chaotic, because the mess is intended to yank us out of our self-sufficiency and self-obsession to become people who really do love God and our neighbors. God puts broken people next to broken people (including leaders), not so they would be comfortable with one another but so they would function as agents of transformation in the lives of one another.

You simply won't have joy in being part of this plan unless you find joy in living a lifestyle of self-denial and willing servanthood.

We complain about the hardships, hassles, workload, and demands of ministry leadership because we are too important to ourselves. We care too much about our own comfort. We keep track of the sacrifices we have to make. We grouse about our lack of control over our schedules. We notice too much how others are responding to us. We fantasize too often about taking a break. We are too easily hurt, too easily discouraged, too easily burdened, and too easily live on the edge of burnout. So we want greater power and control, that is, greater sovereignty over our ministry lives than a servant will ever have.

As a leader, you are not called to mastery; you're called to servanthood. The master who called you didn't live the entitled life of a master but the life of a suffering servant. Every moment of his life, from the straw piercing his infant skin to the nails piercing his hands and feet, your master suffered. Every leadership community is called to follow the mentality, attitudes, submission, and willingness of the servant master who called, equipped, and sent them. Self-focused leadership results in demotivating discontentment, desire for control, and a loss of joy—all of which is an indicator of a fundamental misunderstanding of the position and lifestyle to which you have been called. I want to say here, as I have said in previous chapters, that servant calling and the heart struggle it ignites need to be part of the regular conversation of every ministry leadership community.

Take time with your leadership community to reflect on the following verses and ask yourselves if they describe the mentality, the attitudes, the relationships, and the ministry functionality of the leaders in your community.

They left the presence of the council, rejoicing that they were counted worthy to suffer dishonor for the name. (Acts 5:41)

I will show him how much he must suffer for the sake of my name. (Acts 9:16, of God's call to Paul through Ananias)

The Spirit himself bears witness with our spirit that we are children of God, and if children, then heirs—heirs of God and fellow heirs with Christ, provided we suffer with him in order that we may also be glorified with him. (Rom. 8:16–17)

As it is written, "For your sake we are being killed all the day long; we are regarded as sheep to be slaughtered." (Rom. 8:36)

Our hope for you is unshaken, for we know that as you share in our sufferings, you will also share in our comfort. (2 Cor. 1:7)

Are they servants of Christ? I am a better one—I am talking like a madman—with far greater labors, far more imprisonments, with countless beatings, and often near death. (2 Cor. 11:23)

For his sake I have suffered the loss of all things and count them as rubbish, in order that I may gain Christ and be found in him, not having a righteousness of my own that comes from the law, but that which comes through faith in Christ, the righteousness from God that depends on faith—that I may know him and the power of his resurrection, and may share his sufferings, becoming like him in his death. (Phil. 3:8–10)

If we endure, we will also reign with him;
if we deny him, he also will deny us. (2 Tim. 2:12)

. . . choosing rather to be mistreated with the people of God than to enjoy the fleeting pleasures of sin. (Heb. 11:25, of Moses)

As an example of suffering and patience, brothers, take the prophets who spoke in the name of the Lord. (James 5:10)

For what credit is it if, when you sin and are beaten for it, you endure? But if when you do good and suffer for it you endure, this is a gracious thing in the sight of God. (1 Pet. 2:20)

But even if you should suffer for righteousness' sake, you will be blessed. Have no fear of them, nor be troubled, but in your hearts honor Christ the Lord as holy. (1 Pet. 3:14–15)

If anyone suffers as a Christian, let him not be ashamed, but let him glorify God in that name. (1 Pet. 4:16)

After you have suffered a little while, the God of all grace, who has called you to his eternal glory in Christ, will himself restore, confirm, strengthen, and establish you. (1 Pet. 5:10)

Blessed are you when others revile you and persecute you and utter all kinds of evil against you falsely on my account. (Matt. 5:11)

You will be hated by all for my name's sake. But the one who endures to the end will be saved. (Matt. 10:22)

Whoever finds his life will lose it, and whoever loses his life for my sake will find it. (Matt. 10:39)

Everyone who has left houses or brothers or sisters or father or mother or children or lands, for my name's sake, will receive a hundredfold and will inherit eternal life. (Matt. 19:29)

We are fools for Christ's sake, but you are wise in Christ. We are weak, but you are strong. You are held in honor, but we in disrepute. (1 Cor. 4:10)

For what we proclaim is not ourselves, but Jesus Christ as Lord, with ourselves as your servants for Jesus' sake. (2 Cor. 4:5)

For we who live are always being given over to death for Jesus' sake, so that the life of Jesus also may be manifested in our mortal flesh. (2 Cor. 4:11)

For the sake of Christ, then, I am content with weaknesses, insults, hardships, persecutions, and calamities. For when I am weak, then I am strong. (2 Cor. 12:10)

For it has been granted to you that for the sake of Christ you should not only believe in him but also suffer for his sake. (Phil. 1:29)

There is no doubt about it: servanthood is the thematic biblical description of every follower of Jesus Christ. How much more, then, is it true of those who are called to be leaders? I don't know about you, but I find those passages to be both deeply convicting and profoundly encouraging at the same time. These passages immediately expose what a poor servant I am. I hate when things are in my way. I grow quickly impatient with seemingly needless hassles and delay. I wish I could say that I am okay with being challenged, disagreed with, contradicted, or debated. I love predictable weeks and being surrounded by people who appreciate me. I struggle to love people who critique my love.

So I cry out for the help of my Savior, and I want to be surrounded by leaders who are crying out as well. And I marvel, once again, that the Lord would ever use me, that he never thinks it was a mistake to call me, that he is never disgusted with me, and that he greets my struggle with boundless love, incalculable patience, and mercies that are thankfully new every morning. I know too that he hears my longing and is, by grace, molding my heart into a servant shape.

But there is something else beautiful and encouraging to consider. The call to a life of joyful servitude and willing suffering is itself a grace. In calling me to deny myself, God is freeing me from my bondage to me. Self-focus never leads to happiness, it never produces contentment, and it never results in a satisfied heart. The more a leader has himself in focus, the more he thinks about how ministry inconveniences him, and the less he will experience true joy and lasting contentment. The call to servanthood is the tool that your Lord uses to free you from your discouraging and debilitating bondage to you. The call to servanthood is not just for the glory of your Lord and the benefit of others, but it is God's grace to you as a leadership community. This is the upside-down world of ministry calling. The pathway to freedom is servanthood, the pathway to greatness is slavery, and the pathway to deep and lasting joy—joy that people and circumstance cannot take away—is denying yourself. It is only the grace of the Redeemer that will make a ministry leader find joy in the upside-down world of leadership to which he has been called. Leader, have you entered into that joy, or has it been robbed by delusions of mastery?

Now I want to be honest with you here. The gospel of Jesus Christ allows us to be honest about things we hesitate to talk about or want to hide because the things we want to minimize, hide, or deny have been fully addressed by the life, death, and resurrection of Jesus. As I have traveled around the world, and as I am in almost constant conversations with ministry leaders, it is my estimation that many of us aren't doing well with our suffering-servant calling.

Hypercritical theological arrogance is not the fruit of a servant's heart. Looking for people to troll on Twitter is not what occupies the heart of a servant. Pride of accomplishment contradicts servant humility. Disrespect of the vital gifts of women to the health of the body of Christ fails to mirror the servant heart of Jesus. Treating your church or ministry as if it belongs to you denies your servant calling. Resistance in the face of the loving advice, concern, watchfulness, and rebuke of fellow leaders is resistance against your servant position. Exercising your leadership position in a way that is more political than pastoral does not flow from a servant's heart. Treating staff members as if they are there for you rather than together with you serving the Lord happens when you forget your servant calling.

Any dismissive, disrespectful, impatient, angry, bullying behavior is a failure to joyfully embrace the lifestyle of a servant. Ministry leadership conversations that are regularly marked by complaint are the fruit of entitlement, not servanthood. To get mad at little ministry inconveniences when we have been called to follow our Savior in his suffering, demonstrates how easy it is to drift away from what our Master has called us to be and do.

Leaders, this has been a very difficult chapter to write. I write not to condemn but to encourage. The new identity and potential that are ours in Christ tell us we can do better. Not because we are able, but because the one who is with us, for us, and in us is able. His grace offers us the deeply encouraging welcome to fresh starts and new beginnings. There are many things in ministry leadership that we need to confess, repent of, and forever forsake. Grace frees us from hiding, defending, excusing, or rationalizing away things that have no place in the heart and life of a servant of Jesus.

Why is this so important? It's important because at the heart of every hope that the gospel offers us now and in the future is a suffering servant. Without his willingness to humble and deny himself, without his willingness to become a servant, without his willingness to suffer even to death, there would be no forgiveness, there would be no church, there would be no leaders raised up to carry on the gospel mission, and there would be no message to carry. Suffering servanthood is at the very heart of the redemptive story and the gospel message. Shouldn't it also be at the very heart of our gospel mission and functionality as church and ministry leaders? Is it not possible to be on gospel mission yet deny that very mission in the way that we think about and conduct ourselves?

My prayer is that we would be empowered by God's grace to be joyfully willing as leaders to live the suffering-servant gospel that is our reason for existing, in everything we say and do, in the place where the Savior has positioned us.

PRINCIPLE 8

A spiritually healthy leadership community is characterized by the humility of approachability and the courage of loving honesty.

8.

CANDOR

I GOT THE ANXIOUS CALL from a member of a board, probably because I had written *Dangerous Calling*, so he thought I would be knowledgeable, understanding, and safe.[1] He didn't need to tell me why he was calling; I knew from the emergency nature of the call and the nervousness in his voice that the senior pastor had blown up in some way. What I didn't know was that this conversation and my subsequent involvement in the crisis would be the seedbed in which this book would grow.

The senior pastor had just led the church's annual meeting. There were exciting things happening in the church and in the way it was impacting the surrounding community. The finances were solid, and the future looked bright. He had communicated well and had led the question-and-answer time that followed with a listening ear and helpful answers. The meeting had taken place on a Saturday night, with a dinner and plenty of time for fellowship. On Sunday

---

1. Paul David Tripp, *Dangerous Calling: Confronting the Unique Challenges of Pastoral Ministry* (Wheaton, IL: Crossway, 2012).

morning he had announced a new sermon series and carefully laid out the biblical journey that the church would be taking together. It all seemed to portray a good leader of a good church who was doing the good things God had designed for him to do.

The man who called me described in detail what then happened on Monday night when the board got together for a leadership debrief from the annual meeting and to discuss some other logistics. As the meeting was about to begin, the senior pastor seemed a bit nervous and ill at ease, but no one made much of it. One of his fellow leaders had led in prayer and then turned the meeting over to him, but rather than jumping into the planned debrief, he spoke with great emotion and like someone who is lifting a weighty burden off his chest.

He said, "I just can't do this anymore. I don't want to preach any more sermons. I don't want to lead any more meetings. I don't want to talk to anyone else about their problems. I'm not even sure that I want to be married. In case you're wondering, I haven't cheated on my wife, and I haven't embezzled any of the church's money. I'm just done, and I'm not going to continue to put myself through this. I hate what I'm doing. I find it burdensome and exhausting, and I cannot imagine continuing to do it. I have no plan other than doing what I am doing right now—quitting. I can't tell you how relieved I am that tomorrow I won't be a pastor anymore. I don't want to talk to you about this. I don't want you to pray over me, and I won't go to a counselor. I know you'll want to help, but I don't want help. I want to be left alone and to be free to move on. If you cut me off financially, it won't stop me. I'm done and there is nothing that will undo that."

He continued, "In case you're wondering, I still believe in the Bible and in the work of Jesus Christ, but I no longer believe that I should be in ministry. My marriage is bad, bad enough that I can't imagine continuing that either. My wife is not at fault; it's just that the relationship also has become tiring and burdensome, and I'm just done hoping and trying. I don't know where I'll go, and I don't know what I'll do, but there is one thing I am sure of—I will never be a pastor again, here or anywhere else."

With those words he got up and walked out. One of his fellow leaders followed him down the hallway and out the door and to his car, begging him along the way to come back and talk some more and let them respond, but the pastor said nothing, got into his car, and drove away. The man who went after him came back into the meeting room with tears in his eyes, to a group of shocked and silent leaders. The board member who called me said that they had not heard from him since. He would not take their calls. He had never reentered the church building, and he was living separately from his wife.

I knew the burning question they would ask me would be, "What do we do now?" but that was not the question that haunted me after I got off the phone. My question was, "What is it about this leader and the leadership community that allowed this to happen?" It is very clear that the sad and painful drama of that Monday night was not an isolated event but the end of a dark, lonely, and debilitating process. This senior pastor had been carrying his burden for a long time. He had been struggling to pull off the duties of his calling for a long time. He and his wife had been struggling for a long time. He had not enjoyed preaching for a long time. He had disliked ministry meetings for a long time. He had fantasized about another life for a long time. He had considered different ways to make his escape many times. He had become skilled at hiding his angst while doing his job. He gave a thousand nonanswers to people's questions and was good at putting on a public face. But his skill at hiding just deepened his anguish.

All of this had grown and developed as he was in regular contact with fellow leaders. They were together in formal meetings, in ministry situations, in casual conversations in the hallway, and in times of fellowship. He had been with his leadership community on weekend leadership retreats, at leadership conferences, and during short-term missionary work. Every board meeting began with a catered dinner, accompanied by robust conversation around the table and a time of personal conversation and prayer. Yet what he told them on the fateful Monday night came as a complete shock.

This story is not just about a leader who lost his way but about a ministry leadership community that somehow, someway did not provide what he needed when he needed it most. How did an intimate, seemingly knowledgeable ministry life end with a shocking personal revelation? How did this ministry community not know the man they thought they knew? Let me say again, as I've written before: an isolated, independent, separated, and self-hiding Christian life is alien to the Christianity of the New Testament. Biblical Christianity is thoroughly and foundationally relational. No one can live outside the essential ministries of the body of Christ and remain spiritually healthy. No one is so spiritually mature that he is free from a need for the comfort, warnings, encouragement, rebuke, instruction, and insights of others. Everyone needs partners in struggles. Everyone needs to be helped to see what they cannot see about themselves on their own. This includes leaders. It's not enough to just do leadership activities together, because there is not a moment in time when every leader is free from the need of gospel community. Every leader, to be spiritually healthy, needs spiritual help—every one.

As I walked with these leaders through this dramatic and difficult situation, it made me begin to wonder how many pastor/leaders are hiding things that need to be communicated and that can't be successfully hidden for very long. I began to wonder how many leaders look at their leadership community and simply don't believe that they can speak with complete personal candor and ever get through it together. I wonder how many leaders have made such a mess of things private and corporate that it seems impossible to believe that the leaders around them will respond to the mess with grace and offer to help clean it up. It made me wonder how many church and ministry leaders don't really like their wives and have adversarial relationships with their children but don't think it's possible to admit it to fellow leaders. It made me wonder how leadership communities function together in such a way that allows members to be practically unknown and to suffer alone.

You would think that a struggling leader in trouble would look around at the leaders in the room with him and say, "These are people like me. They know what it means to struggle. They understand discouragement, and they know we all make sinful choices. I know these leaders love me. I know they will work to comfort, rescue, restore, and encourage me. These leaders offer me a safe place to be real, honest, and self-disclosing. I can speak and not be afraid." You would think this would be the case, but it is not. We hesitate and delay, not just because we are self-protective or like our sin but also because we are not sure that our ministry leadership community will love us with gospel love in those moments when we need it most. A spiritually healthy leadership community is spiritually healthy when it is a safe place for struggling leaders to speak with candor and hope.

LEADERSHIP CANDOR: A BIBLICAL CASE STUDY

I want to examine with you a biblical example of the kind of candor I am pleading for here and its results. Read carefully the words of the apostle Paul that follow.

> Blessed be the God and Father of our Lord Jesus Christ, the Father of mercies and God of all comfort, who comforts us in all our affliction, so that we may be able to comfort those who

are in any affliction, with the comfort with which we ourselves are comforted by God. For as we share abundantly in Christ's sufferings, so through Christ we share abundantly in comfort too. If we are afflicted, it is for your comfort and salvation; and if we are comforted, it is for your comfort, which you experience when you patiently endure the same sufferings that we suffer. Our hope for you is unshaken, for we know that as you share in our sufferings, you will also share in our comfort.

For we do not want you to be unaware, brothers, of the affliction we experienced in Asia. For we were so utterly burdened beyond our strength that we despaired of life itself. Indeed, we felt that we had received the sentence of death. But that was to make us rely not on ourselves but on God who raises the dead. He delivered us from such a deadly peril, and he will deliver us. On him we have set our hope that he will deliver us again. You also must help us by prayer, so that many will give thanks on our behalf for the blessing granted us through the prayers of many. (2 Cor. 1:3–11)

I have provided context for you, but what I'm really interested in, for our discussion, is the second paragraph. Pay careful attention to how Paul talks about his difficult situation. He seems to have no desire to be self-protective. The ministry leaders I regularly meet with often share a personal experience, but they leave out how they themselves factor into it. They talk about what happened and what other people did and said, but they give me little sense of their own heart struggle as it was all going on. I find that I have to pry a bit to get to the spiritual struggle behind the situational difficulty.

Now, you know that even the best of ministry leaders do not always do well. You know that sometimes they get discouraged by difficulties at home or in their ministry. You know that there are moments when they struggle with impatience, anger, frustration, or envy. You know that not every ministry leader around the table

experiences regular joy in the Lord and in his service. You know that
ministry leaders get burdened by ministry responsibilities and the
busyness that follows. You know that ministry leaders are tempted
to give way to thoughts and desires that they should not entertain
or follow. Yet, seldom in our ministry communities do we talk about
these things.

Now back to Paul. In the passage above, Paul describes not just
the hard situation; he speaks with candor about the heart struggle
it initiated. How more candid, how more humbly honest and self-
disclosing, could you get than these words: "For we were so utterly
burdened beyond our strength that we despaired of life itself. . . . We
felt that we had received the sentence of death" (vv. 8–9). It's hard to
think of these desperate words coming from the mouth of Paul. Here
he is, the giant of the gospel; Paul, who exegeted our faith for us;
Paul, our example of the transforming power of the gospel—revealing his experience of utter despair. Paul, yes, the apostle Paul, went
through a situation in which he thought, "This is it; it's over." Yes,
it is true that Paul was a man just like us. Paul was a man capable of
spiritual despair. Paul was not free from frailty of heart, nor am I,
nor is any leader reading this book. But remarkable here, given the
ministry leadership culture that most of us live and work in, is that
Paul has no hesitancy, no problem, sharing the depth of the struggle
of his heart.

Leader, are you comfortable with this level of personal candor?
Does your leadership community welcome confessions of weakness
and struggle? Are there subtle, unspoken ways that you look down
on leaders who are weak? Does your leadership culture silence confessions of struggle? Does the way you define a leader forbid leaders
from confessing places of doubt and despair? Is your community so
rich in patient love and gospel care that each leader feels comfortable with the kind of candor that is needed for long-term spiritual
health? Do you hide your true self from your fellow leaders, and

do you think others do too? Has your leadership community had candid moments followed by encouragement, comfort, promises of assistance, warning, and prayer? Do you really know the leaders around the table whom you think you know? What in the way you relate and function as a leadership community would cause a leader to be afraid to be open and honest about personal heart struggles?

It is quite possible to be committed to leading robust gospel ministries and yet be denying the same gospel in your leadership community. Hiding in fear, silence, denial, defensiveness, and a vacuum of humble candor is more of the culture of broken Eden than of victorious Calvary. At the heart of the wonderful new and radically different life that we are welcomed to, based on the person and sacrifice of Jesus, is the welcome to confession. We are lovingly called out of the darkness, out from behind the trees into the open and the light, not because we don't have things to hide but because grace means we no longer have to hide them. The one from whom we have hidden is now our Father, and the things we hid have been fully atoned for. And it is very clear in the New Testament that the vertical freedom that God has given us to be humbly honest with him is meant to shape the way we live and relate to one another. Because we can be honest with God, we can also be honest with one another. That's why James boldly says, "Confess your sins to one another and pray for one another, that you may be healed" (James 5:16).

A gospel-shaped leadership community will be a confessional community, where leader honesty is a not only a constant protection but encourages a deeper and deeper dependency on God. Confessing communities tend to be humble communities. Confessing communities tend to be worshiping communities. Confessing communities tend to be praying communities. Leaders who confess tend to be tender and kind when people they are called to lead mess up and need to confess. The more a leader has the joy of being in a confessing community, the more he will come to see his need for grace, and because he does, he will tend to be a giver of that same grace. In a confessing leadership community, leaders' pride shrinks and worship of God grows.

It is in the soil of the devastation and humiliation of confession that servant leaders grow. In the pain of personal candor, lust for power wanes and passion for the gospel grows. Was this not the result in Paul's life? The passage ends with a deeper dependency on God and humble community prayer. This is the culture that every leadership community needs to foster and encourage. How can we lead people into the welcome of the gospel if we are not living in that welcome as a leadership community? How can we call people out of hiding if we are hiding? How can we call them to deal with things we are still denying? How can we encourage them to confess when we are afraid to confess? How can we call them to love one another, no matter what, when we are not doing the same as a leadership community? How can we invite people to have complete confidence in the gospel when our leadership culture is subtly shaped by a functional lack of confidence in the same? Leaders, the gospel of Jesus Christ predicts that we can do better.

WHAT SILENCES US?

Why isn't humble candor more of a regular part of our ministry leadership culture? Why aren't we more ready to confess spiritual discouragement or struggle? Why do we sit in silence as we watch fellow leaders drift away from the type of people God calls them to be? Why are too many of us more defensive than approachable? Why do we seem to be more concerned about and activated by the sin of others than we are by our own? What silences humble gospel candor in our leadership communities? Well, I want to suggest a few answers to these questions. My hope is that it will prompt community self-examination and discussion.

1. Pride of Personal Maturity

Pride is a huge issue for all ministry leaders. Knowledge gets to us, experience gets to us, success gets to us, position gets to us, increasing notoriety gets to us, and in so doing we are placed in spiritual danger. Pride is a temptation that every leadership community should be aware of and keep a watchful eye on. Sadly, way too many leaders change throughout the life of their ministry leadership. The humble, gracious, servant attitude wanes as knowledge, success, and prominence increase. We hear it in the way leaders talk about themselves and how they talk about and relate to others.

If ministry knowledge, experience, success, and position have begun to distort your sense of yourself, if they have caused you to forget who you really are and what you daily need, you will not be quick to admit your sin, weaknesses, and failures to yourself or to others. Pride and confession are enemies. They do not work in cooperation but in constant opposition. If ministry has come to define you, the gospel won't. Perhaps many leaders are silent because they have fallen into the delusion that they don't really have anything to confess or don't see where they need the pastoral love and assistance of fellow leaders.

2. Ability to Minimize Sin

It is one of the most powerful aspects of the scary and destructive deceitfulness of sin. As long as sin is inside us, we all carry with us a dangerous ability to participate in our own spiritual blindness. It should be a warning to every leadership community everywhere that all members of your community are regularly tempted to think that their sin is something less than sin. We're able to name our anger as zeal for what is right. We are skilled at calling our impatience a desire to move forward with gospel mission. We are tempted to call gossip the sharing of prayer concerns. Being power and control hungry gets recast as exercising God-given leadership gifts.

Every leadership community needs to pray together for grace to see sin as dark, despicable, destructive, and dishonoring to God as it actually is. Every leadership community needs to regularly cry out for help, admitting that sin doesn't always look sinful. We need to seek divine rescue from our ability to erect self-atoning arguments for our righteousness that crush gospel grief and humble confession. Any leadership community that has become individually or corporately comfortable with minimizing sin is, because of that, in real and present spiritual danger.

3. Must Have the Respect of Others

It is my temptation, and if you're a leader, it's your temptation too: we care too much about what fellow leaders think of us. There are times when I give more of the concern of my heart to the opinion of a particular ministry colleague than to the view of my Lord. I want too much to be respected. I want too much to be liked. I am too concerned with being spoken well of. I overly desire that fellow leaders affirm my ideas and give weight to my plans. I am too attentive to how fellow leaders respond to me. I am greatly tempted, as is every leader in some way, to care too much about what others think of me.

Balanced relationships in a leadership community are a tricky thing for which we need much grace. On one hand, I am in hand-to-hand spiritual war with my fellow leaders, so we need to have a relationship of respect and trust. One the other hand, I cannot let their acceptance and respect be what controls how I relate to them. If I care too much about what they think of me, I will put forth my strengths while hiding my weaknesses and failures. If I have them in the appropriate place in my heart, I will see them as God-given tools of grace and be free to be candid with them about my real issues of heart and life. Every leadership community needs to pray for grace to get this balance right.

4. Identity in Ministry

If ministry leadership is your identity, then Christ isn't, along with that life-changing catalog of comforts that are the result of his person and work. Ministry leadership identity produces fear and anxiety and will never produce the humility and courage that come with identity in Christ. Looking horizontally, as a leader, for your identity, meaning, purpose, and internal sense of well-being asks people, places, and position to do for you what only your Messiah can do. This will produce either pride in success or fear of failure but never the kind of humility and courage of heart that results in humble, willing, confessing approachability. Ministry as a source of identity will never result in healthy gospel-shaped relationships in your leadership community, the kind of relationships in which candor is encouraged, confession is greeted with grace, and bonds of love, appreciation, affection, understanding, and respect grow strong.

5. Functional Gospel Doubt

Yes, it is possible to be part of a leadership community that has the gospel as its central message and the spread of the gospel as its central mission but whose leaders are silenced by gospel doubt. Too many leaders struggling with issues in their hearts, lives, and relationships have their responses shaped more by a catalog of doubtful "what ifs" than by the hope-producing promises of the gospel. Leaders can't imagine how their confession will turn out well, so they hide behind silence, denials, or nonanswers. Rather than being thankful for the ever-present grace that is theirs in Christ and the community of grace that surrounds them, they doubt rescuing and forgiving grace and fear the very people tasked with being tools of that grace.

The gospel is laden with promises of forgiveness and restoration. The gospel offers us the comfort of fresh starts and new beginnings. The gospel promises us that the good things God calls us to will produce good in our lives, even if that good looks different from what we hoped for. The gospel reminds us that hardship in the hands of the Lord is a tool of rescuing, forgiving, transforming, and delivering grace. The gospel tells us that Jesus measured up in every way because we wouldn't and that he took the Father's rejection so we would never have to. Here's what every leadership community needs to affirm: to come out of hiding produces good, to admit what you have denied produces good, to confess sin produces good, to own where you are weak produces good, and to say no to pride and cry out for help, even if there is wreckage along the way, produces good.

Will we allow ourselves to esteem ministry identity and position more than we esteem a humble and clean heart before the Lord and in relationship to the fellow leaders he has placed us near? Do we fear loss of a leadership position more than we fear giving sin room to do its evil work in our hearts and lives? Do we really believe that our Redeemer is kind, tender, loving, and good? Do we really believe that all his ways are right and true? Will we allow ourselves to think that his way is more dangerous than our way? Will we let functional gospel doubt silence us when our Savior is calling us to confess and be healed?

This has been a tough and convicting chapter to write. It has caused me to examine why it is hard for me in places to say, "I was wrong; please forgive me." It has required me to ask myself why at times I find it hard to own my weaknesses and seek help. And it has deepened my longing to be in a robust gospel community with other leaders, where we know we are loved and will find grace, where we know we are needy, and where humble candor is the culture, not the exception. For this, every leader needs grace, and that grace is ours, operating now and secure because of the life, death, and resurrection of our fellow leader, companion, and friend—the Lamb, the Lord, the Savior, Jesus. It is only by his power that our fears are silenced and our mouths are filled with humility, hope, confession, and praise. May we rest in him, and in resting, come out of the hiding and speak. And in speaking, may we experience good things from him that are way better than the bad things we feared.

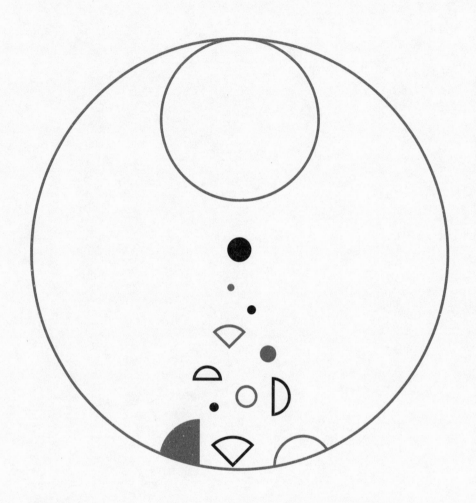

PRINCIPLE 9

Where your leaders look for identity always
determines how they lead.

— 9. —

IDENTITY

I SAT IN THE MEETING. I was the new guy, and I couldn't believe what I was hearing. This leader who I looked up to and wanted to be like was confessing stuff I wouldn't have thought of confessing. He was telling the people around the table about a person whom he was called to lead and love but instead had come to loathe. He had developed such antipathy toward this person that he dreaded seeing him, only tolerated talking to him, and complained about him. I was shocked, not because I thought this leader was perfect but because he wasn't afraid of admitting his imperfection to the fellow leaders he worked with every day.

My response was, "No way!" I had just arrived on scene. I wanted the people around the table to think well of me and to trust me, so there was no way I was going to be so self-disclosing. I was more focused on building an identity than sharing my heart. I said almost nothing during that meeting, but I sat in my office with an unsettled heart. There was a war going on inside me, a war of desire. I was delighted to have been offered a seat around the table. It was more than

I thought I would ever achieve in ministry. I was overwhelmed that I was now a colleague of leaders I had looked up to for some years. I didn't want to be the weak one. I wanted to be strong, a contributor on par with the other leaders in the room. But I also knew if pride in position controlled my heart, I would not run to the graces of the gospel or the help and protection of the gospel community around me. Rooting my identity in ministry leadership would cause me to hide important details about myself, control conversations, compete for position, deny weaknesses while projecting strength, and a host of other spiritual dangers.

I am thankful that God arranged that I would be confronted in that very first meeting with the danger of getting my identity from ministry leadership. So I want to expand the conversation of this point, which we began in the last chapter. Getting our identity from ministry is not only a dangerous and miserable ministry experience, but also disrupts the kind of ministry community that we need and that serves the spiritual health of fellow leaders.

LET'S TALK ABOUT IDENTITY

I want to take time to develop a bit of a biblical theology of identity with the hope that it will argue for the importance of this issue and its impact on the spiritual health and functionality of any ministry leadership community. This Bible is rife with identity statements and terminology: *creature, Creator, male, female, child, parents, son, daughter, Son of God, children of God, Master, disciple, body of Christ, strangers and aliens,* and the list goes on and on. Thinking about identity and the identities that we assign to ourselves is a significant part of our rationality. You see, we are wired by God to be constant interpreters. Everything we do every day is rooted in fundamental interpretations about who God is and who we are, about right and wrong, about meaning and purpose, about relationships, and about

motivation, and this is just a suggestive list of the long list of interpretations that shape the way we see, think, choose, act, and speak.

This means that none of us, from the most influential leader
down to the least influential follower, responds to life based on the
pure facts of our existence. Rather, all our responses are the result
of how we have interpreted those facts. That is precisely why there
can be two leaders in the same organization who have very different
responses to the same set of circumstantial facts. We'll never stop
interpreting, because we were wired by God to search for meaning
and understanding. We all have a deep desire to make sense out of
life. All this was wired inside us by God to drive us to him so that he
would live at the center of the way we understand ourselves, understand life, and make sense out of our circumstances.

In one of my very first books, *Instruments in the Redeemer's
Hands*,[1] I wrote that this is why God, after creating Adam and Eve,
began to talk to them. Without God, they would not have known
how to make proper sense out of life. In the garden, God gave them
the foundational elements of a Godward interpretive structure so
that they could make valid interpretations of life on the ground. For
example, understanding "creature" as a basic piece of your identity
changes everything. If I have been created by someone, then that
someone had a purpose in mind for making me, so understanding
that purpose is vital to my proper functioning.

I've already begun to hint at it, but let me just say it: there may be
no more important and life-shaping interpretation that human beings make than identity. In God's perfect plan, the man and woman
he made and their children and their children's children were meant
to get their foundational sense of identity vertically. This is how they
were meant to know themselves, how they would understand their
meaning and purpose, and how they would find that inner sense of

---

1. Paul David Tripp, *Instruments in the Redeemer's Hands: People in Need of Change Helping
People in Need of Change*, Resources for Changing Lives (Phillipsburg, NJ: P&R, 2002), n.p.

well-being that every person wants. This vertical identity was to give them guidance for their daily living and erect protective boundaries around their hearts. So the disobedience of Adam and Eve was profoundly more than the eating of forbidden food. It was a rejection of their identity as creatures of the Most High God and buying into an identity that did not have God at the center. And with that sad rejection, human identity became not only a morass of confusion but the battleground for spiritual war.

Since the fall, people look horizontally for what they were designed to find vertically. They ask people, places, and things to do for them what only identity in the Lord can do. And what people fail to understand is that wherever you look for identity will then exercise rulership over your heart and, in so doing, will direct the way you live your life. Things that were never meant to be sources of human identity become just that, creating endless layers of difficulty and brokenness.

A job is a wonderful provision from God, but if it becomes your identity, it will leave you regularly unhappy and will destroy your family. Your marriage is a significant human relationship, but if it becomes your identity, you will ask your spouse to be your personal messiah, placing on your spouse a burden that he or she will never be able to bear. Your body is a significant aspect of who you are, but if you look to it as your primary source of identity, then aging, weakness, or disease will rob you of your sense of self. Depression is a deeply personal and powerful emotional experience, but if you take it on as your identity, it will do you even further spiritual and emotional harm. There is always the temptation this side of eternity to look for identity horizontally, but looking there never delivers what you seek and never results in a harvest of good fruit.

This is why the New Testament works to instill in every believer an identity in Christ and to exegete what that looks like in terms of the way we think about and approach our everyday lives. Check just a few New Testament examples:

> Therefore, if anyone is in Christ, he is a new creation. The old has passed away; behold, the new has come. (2 Cor. 5:17)

> You are a chosen race, a royal priesthood, a holy nation, a people for his own possession, that you may proclaim the excellencies of him who called you out of darkness into his marvelous light. (1 Pet. 2:9)

> I have been crucified with Christ. It is no longer I who live, but Christ who lives in me. And the life I now live in the flesh I live by faith in the Son of God, who loved me and gave himself for me. (Gal. 2:20)

> No longer do I call you servants, for the servant does not know what his master is doing; but I have called you friends, for all that I have heard from my Father I have made known to you. (John 15:15)

> To all who did receive him, who believed in his name, he gave the right to become children of God. (John 1:12)

> The Spirit himself bears witness with our spirit that we are children of God, and if children, then heirs—heirs of God and fellow heirs with Christ, provided we suffer with him in order that we may also be glorified with him. (Rom. 8:16–17)

> You have died, and your life is hidden with Christ in God. (Col. 3:3)

> In Christ Jesus you are all sons of God, through faith. (Gal. 3:26)

> There is therefore now no condemnation for those who are in Christ Jesus. (Rom. 8:1)

Our citizenship is in heaven, and from it we await a Savior, the Lord Jesus Christ. (Phil. 3:20)

Now you are the body of Christ and individually members of it. (1 Cor. 12:27)

Do you not know that your body is a temple of the Holy Spirit within you, whom you have from God? You are not your own, for you were bought with a price. So glorify God in your body. (1 Cor. 6:19–20)

We are his workmanship, created in Christ Jesus for good works, which God prepared beforehand, that we should walk in them. (Eph. 2:10)

Put on the new self, created after the likeness of God in true righteousness and holiness. (Eph. 4:24)

It is very clear from these passages, and many more, that identity in Christ is intended to be the defining element in the way that a believer makes sense out of who he is and what he is supposed to be doing. Any other identity will unsettle his heart, expose him to various idolatries, ask of creation what it cannot give, and cause him to step outside of God's wise and loving boundaries. Because identity is the ground of how we make sense of life, it is both a spiritual war and one of the ways the gospel gives us back our sanity and security.

Now, I am aware that what I have just taken the time to lay out for you is, for most ministry leaders, not so much a body of new insights but a review. I have taken the time so that you would reflect on the significance of this issue, particularly as it applies to the ongoing spiritual health of a ministry leadership community. Every leader in every leadership community is doing his or her work out of some sense of identity. It is neither accurate nor safe to assume that ministry leaders always function, at street level, out of their identity in Christ. A ministry leader's identity is a place of temptation and a spiritual battleground and, sadly, does not always remain constant. It is clear to me that a significant aspect of the drift and then fall of ministry leaders begins with an identity exchange. This exchange is not a dramatic event but rather a subtle and often long-term process.

Likely no one goes into ministry saying, "I am going to make ministry my identity," but along the way, something happens. The things that we have talked about throughout this book, which are the fruit of heeding Christ's call and surrendering gifts for his use, begin to become identity markers. Theological expertise; detailed biblical knowledge; years of ministry experience; success; the acceptance, respect, and love of people; and the strengths of one's gifts and the power of influence and position begin to be where a leader looks to know who he is. It is incredibly ironic that the fruit of a leader's identity in Christ is what tempts him to look elsewhere for identity. Somewhere, without a conscious rejection of his gospel theology, he has exchanged the stability of vertical identity for the instability of horizontal identity. Because he has made this exchange, his heart is exposed to a variety of ministry idolatries (e.g., knowledge, power, control, position, success, acclaim, lifestyle ease), and he is not the same person and does not function in the same way that he did in the early days of his ministry.

This is happening right now to leaders all around us. How can we not be concerned about this dynamic? How can it not be part of our regular conversation as leaders as we try to protect one another and maintain the spiritual health of our leadership communities? How can we not examine the sins of our own hearts and the conduct of our lives, seeking to know if there is evidence that we too have made that dangerous exchange? Ministry leadership really is a miserable, spiritually dangerous, and leader-destroying place to look for identity. Nothing good is produced in a leader who has along the way exchanged identity in Christ for some form of identity in ministry.

A PROFILE OF A LEADER WHO HAS MADE
THE IDENTITY EXCHANGE

If identity in ministry is a battleground for every ministry leader, and if the exchange from identity in Christ to identity in ministry is often subtle and usually takes place over an extended period of time, then it is important to identify some of the symptoms you will see when a leader is looking to get from his ministry leadership what he was meant to get from Christ. Following is a suggestive, but surely not exhaustive, list.

Fear

When you look horizontally for your sense of self, your daily worth, your reason for keeping on, and your inner rest and security, you are all too attentive to the opinions, responses, reactions, and situations around you. You look too intensely at how people are responding to you, and you listen too carefully to what people are saying and how they say it. You notice discussions or plans that have included you. You are troubled by the advancement of others and quietly envious of their ministry successes. Your hyperattentiveness crushes your peace of heart, leaving worry, concern, anxiety, and/or fear in its place. It is a vicious cycle, because the more you pay attention, the more you find reason to be concerned, and the more you're concerned, the more you pay attention. It is spiritually defeating, relationally unhealthy, and motivationally paralyzing. The reason you're experiencing fear is that you're asking ministry leadership to give you what it was not designed to and is not able to give. In your position as a ministry leader, you have been called to be an ambassador of the Savior, but that leadership position cannot give you what the Savior alone is able to give.

Ministry success won't give you the well-being you're looking for, because ministry successes are often followed by failures. People's appreciation and respect won't offer you the worth you seek, because the person who praised you today will criticize you tomorrow. The esteem of busy fellow leaders won't deliver the spiritual wholeness you crave. No other leader is able to function as your personal messiah, because he or she is in the battle too. The buzz of position is fleeting, soon giving way to the burden of responsibility. When you look horizontally for what you have already been given vertically, the things you look to will always fail you.

There are too many leaders among us who do too many things out of fear and not faith. Too many of us are anxiously driven. Too many of us are too moved by the criticism of others. Too many of us care too much about our opinions winning the day, our sermons being applauded, or about people liking us. Too many of us, in the suffering that is the life of every ministry leader, are not suffering well. Too many of us develop negative attitudes toward people we are called to minister with or to, because we overly need them to appreciate and cooperate with us. Looking horizontally for our identity and peace is burdensome, exhausting, and self-defeating. For some of us, it will make us fantasize about moving to another ministry leadership place or quitting altogether.

There are times when I have looked too intently, listened too hard, let someone get to me, and felt discouragement wash over me. All of this has happened as Jesus was loving me, showering me with his grace, fulfilling all his promises to me, blessing me with gifts, calling me to be part of his redemptive mission, and providing for me with his enabling, protecting, transforming, and delivering grace. That means that in those moments, as a ministry leader I had lost my gospel mind. Because I had lost my mind, I gave in to the insanity of feeling poor and searching to be fed, when actually I was rich and well supplied.

Pride

When it comes to identity in ministry, fear and pride have the same root. Although the fear and pride can have very different manifestations, the same in either case is a leader looking where he should not look for something that has already been supplied. When you look to your ministry leadership for worth, security, and a reason to continue, you need your ministry to deliver. So not only are you hyperattentive and aware, but you also take credit for what you could never earn, produce, or achieve on your own. A leader's struggle with pride is often connected to the identity exchange we have been discussing.

Because a leader needs his ministry position to give him what it was never meant to give, he needs to see himself as more essential than he actually is. And because he looks to ministry to give him his sense of worth, he is tempted to assign to himself more power to produce results than any leader will ever have. In his search for spiritual rest and stability, he again and again does poor spiritual math, adding two and two and getting five. No leader has the power to create change. No leader is able to determine results. No leader can control the response of people, let alone the flow of events. No leader has the ability to soften hearts, to make them faithful, humble, and courageous. No leader can control the opinions of fellow leaders. No leader can cause people to hunger for the gospel. No leader is a change agent; rather, every ministry leader is a tool in the toolbox of the one who alone holds the power of change in his hands.

A leader's pride in ministry achievement is not only a self-serving delusion; it is redemptive thievery, taking personal pride in what only the Redeemer can do. It is a thin bubble that will soon break, because it is not true, and it does not give the spiritual nutrients that every leader needs.

Emotional Highs and Lows

The truths of the gospel, that is, the radical realities of the presence, promises, power, love, and grace of the Savior, are the only rock of stability for a ministry leader. It really is true and needs to be said again and again: all other ground is sinking sand. For all the high mountains of ministry leadership, there are many dark valleys. For all the people who love and appreciate you, there are people who misunderstand and misjudge you. For all the wonderful moments of unity, there are moments when it seems as if you've been torn asunder. For all the times you feel prepared and able, there are times you are faced with your weakness and inadequacy. For all the leadership things you delight in doing, there are those you hate doing. For all the seasons of joy, there are seasons of sorrow. Such is the inescapable ebb and flow of ministry leadership.

Your ministry cannot give you the peace that passes understanding, but Jesus can. Your ministry cannot offer you unbroken love, but Jesus does. Your leadership position cannot give you courage in the darkness, but the Savior, who walks with you, will. Your ministry leadership does not always make you feel worthy, but the one who shed his blood for you will. Your ministry cannot satisfy your hungry soul, but the bread of life and living water can. When a ministry leader feeds on spiritual food that cannot satisfy, he has the high of feeling spiritually full for a moment, only to be hungry once again.

Leader, you will never experience long-term spiritual health and stability when you look to your ministry position and function to give you what the Savior has promised you and is delivering to you. I am convinced that emotional volatility and instability in leadership are often rooted in the identity exchange we have been examining.

Control

The most controlling people I have counseled or worked with have always proven to be the most fearful. When you look somewhere for what you weren't meant to find there, you tend to be afraid, and the way to assuage your fear is to control what needs to be controlled in order to best guarantee that you find what you're looking for. Psalm 112:7 says of the righteous man:

> He is not afraid of bad news;
>> his heart is firm, trusting in the LORD.

I love those words. A leader whose identity and security is in the Lord is liberated from fear, even in the face of bad news. His heart is firm, not wobbly, unstable, or weak. He is not fear-free because he is in control. He is not fear-free because he has nothing to fear. He is fear-free because he gets his stability, his sense of well-being, vertically. He does not need to be in control, because he does not need the things around him to go well for his heart to be firm.

Every leader in every leadership community is either resting in the complete and perfect control of the heavenly Father over every person and every situation or seeking to take control. Every leader is looking for firmness of heart either vertically or horizontally, and when you look horizontally you crave more control over people, plans, and circumstances than any leader was meant or qualified to have. Desire for control is a symptom of fear, and fear is a symptom of trusting a replacement savior who just can't deliver what your heart cries for.

Sensitivity

I have covered sensitivity already, so I won't spend much time on it here. When you need things and people around you to give you what they weren't designed to give, you care too much about responses and results, and because you do, you are way too sensitive to what is happening around you. You take yourself and others way too seriously. You take people's responses as being way more important than they actually are. You care too much about what results say about you, your gifts, your insight, your commitment, and your faithfulness. You tend to take offense where no offense was meant. You tend to personalize what is not personal, drawing personal messages out of events and conversations when nothing personal was there to be found. All of this creates a self-focused seriousness that troubles a leader's relationships and disrupts the spiritual health and unity of the leadership community that surrounds him.

Leaders, is there any evidence in your heart, relationships, or leadership that somewhere along the way this identity exchange has taken place? Is there any way that you're looking horizontally for what you've already been blessed with in Jesus? Is fear, pride, control, or sensitivity an indicator of something you should examine? Do you have a firm heart, one that is secure and at rest? Is ministry leadership a bit of a fearful burden or a joy? You don't need to be afraid of examining your heart, because whatever you find there has already been addressed by the person and work of Jesus.

I want to close this chapter by speaking to those of you who have been discouraged by what you have read. Yes, it is true that a ministry leader's life is messy, but it is God's mess. Your Lord knows the sin and weakness of the people he has chosen to lead his church. He knows there are times when we look to the wrong things for our spiritual stability. He knows that at times we are too fearful, too controlling, too proud, too sensitive, and too needy of affirmation and success. He knows all our susceptibilities, yet he still chose us to lead his people on his redemptive mission. He is not shocked or dismayed by our struggle, and he surely is not about to give up on us. He meets us in our weaknesses, smashes our idols, exposes our hearts, and then draws us near once again and says, "I've called you to my service, not because you are able but because I am. Rest your heart on my grace and don't look elsewhere for what only I can give you." And with those tender, loving words he grants us yet again another fresh start and new beginning.

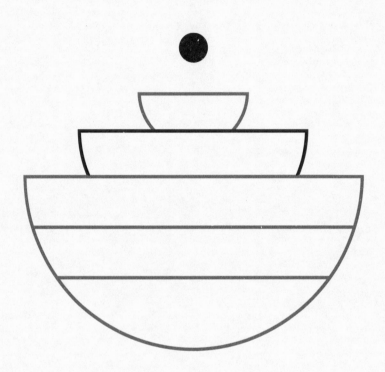

PRINCIPLE 10

*If a leadership community is formed by the gospel, it will
always be committed to a lifestyle of fresh starts
and new beginnings.*

— 10.—

RESTORATION

HE CALLED ME in a bit of a panic because he didn't know who else to call. (He had audited one of my classes.) He was calling because he had found his senior pastor, who was his mentor, in what seemed to be an emotional breakdown. His pastor was irrational, saying things that made no sense. He drove his pastor home, and as the pastor mumbled his way into his house, my former student called and asked me for help. I called his pastor, introduced myself, explained to him why I was calling, and offered my counseling help if it was needed. He thanked me for my concern and told me he had been through a grueling ministry week, hadn't got much sleep, and had had a bit of a physical breakdown. I prayed with him but left the conversation quite concerned and thinking that I would hear from him or someone close to him again.

A few weeks later, I got a phone call from another man I didn't know. He was very upset and said that what he was about to tell me needed immediate action, but it had to be done confidentially. He was reaching out to me after scheduling an appointment with the same senior pastor from a few weeks back. The only time they'd been able to meet was after the senior pastor's normal work hours. By the time the man arrived at the pastor's office, most of the staff had gone home, and he was let into the building by a janitor. He made his way to the pastor's office and knocked on the door, but there was no answer. He hesitated for a moment and then stuck his head in the door opening. He saw the pastor with his head down on the desk and called out to him. Alarmed when he got no response, he went over to shake the pastor to see if he was okay, and the moment he got close, he was hit with the smell of alcohol. He knew right away that his pastor wasn't sick or sleeping; he was drunk.

He ran out of the church building, heart pounding, and called me, because we had developed a bit of a friendship, and he had no idea what to do next. I told him to call the chair of the elder board, which he did. It was like a bomb dropped in the middle of that church. Never had the leadership imagined that such a problem would drop in their lap. Never had they thought that such a thing could be going on in the life of this pastor who was so effective and seemed so committed. Weighty questions swirled around in the minds of the elders about what to do next and what this meant for the life and ministry of the church. And soon it became obvious to me that the developing plan was to set aside the pastor, give him a loving severance, and find a new senior pastor.

Here was a man who had clearly been given ministry, leadership, preaching, and pastoral gifts. Here was a man who had evangelized and discipled many. Here was a preacher-teacher who had given his congregation biblical literacy and theological knowledge, and he was about to be set aside as if he were a commodity, no longer useful and not a dear, God-gifted leader and brother in Christ. The plan seemed more like what an NFL team would do with a weakened player than the actions of a church that believes in the power of rescuing and restoring grace.

I asked if there was any way that I could meet with the elders. My hope was that I could give them an alternative plan. I did my best in the meeting to do two things. First, I preached to these wonderful but scared men of the power and beauty of God's restorative grace and its promise of fresh starts and new beginnings. And then I laid out a possible restoration plan that included elder and diaconal care, elders' wives to care for the fallen pastor's wife, babysitters to be on call as needed, addiction counseling, a system of loving accountability, and ongoing support during the restoration process.

It was a long haul and at times ranged from discouraging to seemingly futile, but God was at work in this process. Through the loving ministry of many, he was restoring this man, reclaiming his gifts, and reshaping his trajectory. No promises were made to the pastor of his return to ministry—only promises of continuing support, help, counsel, and encouragement.

I am so thankful to communicate that this man who had fallen so far has returned to ministry. He is the lead pastor of another church, with a vibrant, growing ministry to its surrounding community. God was not done with him, and the church shouldn't have been either. Leader restoration is not a romantic dream of people who don't really understand how deep and serious sin is. Restoration gets at the heart of the gospel that we have given ourselves to. And even if sin necessitates a leader's removal from his position and ministry duties, turning toward him with grace is always right. We sinners don't just need forgiving grace; we need reconciling grace. And we don't just need reconciling grace; we need restoring grace. And we don't just need restoring grace; we need delivering grace. It is beautiful to see the power of restorative grace up close and personal, and it is sad to see that so many leadership communities don't actually trust its power when a key leader's sin has been revealed by the divine restorer.

EVERYBODY BELIEVES IN GRACE UNTIL A LEADER NEEDS IT

Every church or ministry leadership community must be a restorative community if it's going to have long-term spiritual health and ministry effectiveness. A commitment to the spirit, attitudes, and actions of restoration is vital. As I have written before, there may be nothing more important, humbling, or culture-shaping for a ministry leadership community than to keep in view at all times that every member of the community is in the middle of their own sanctification. No leader is sin free, no leader lives above the great spiritual battle for the focus and rulership of his heart, and no leader has graduated from his need for grace. Every leader fails to live up to God's standard in word, thought, or action somehow, someway, every day. Every leader still has moments when he thinks things that he should not think, desires what he should not desire, and acts or speaks in ways that are wrong.

No leader is impervious to a moment of pride or a flash of lust. No leader is above irritation, anger, jealousy, or impatience. Every leader struggles at some time with fear of man or pride of accomplishment. Ministry leaders are quite capable of disrespecting staff members or looking at the opposite sex in ways that are wrong. No leader has a perfect marriage or is a perfect parent. No leader has completely pure and unmixed motives. Here's the bottom line: no leader in any ministry community anywhere is done, that is, completely formed into the image of Jesus Christ.

So if it is true that every leader is in the middle of the ongoing work of God's sanctifying grace, then it is also true that there is still the presence of remaining sin in every leader's heart. And if there is the presence of remaining sin in their hearts, the leaders will fail, sin, and fall. Sometimes anger robs a leader of his effectiveness. Sometimes envy interrupts the kind of relationships every leader needs for his spiritual health and ministry productivity. Sometimes pride of position and accomplishment gets in the way of the servant posture that must be the stance of every ministry leader. Sometimes private sin grows until the leader is addicted and enslaved. Sometimes a leader flags in his personal pursuit of God and presses ahead in a state of spiritual dryness. Sometimes private family dysfunction or marital unfaithfulness exists right alongside a leader's public ministry. All leaders need spiritual care, but some fall and require loving, firm, well-administered restorative grace.

As I travel the world and have sat with ministry leaders from a wide variety of ecclesiastical and cultural backgrounds, I have seen that when it comes to leaders' struggle with sin, we tend to make unbiblical assumptions that cause us to be naïve and unprepared for battles that we will face in the life and ministry of leaders in our communities. It is not safe to assume that a seminary graduate is spiritually okay. It's not safe to conclude that a very gifted leader is where he needs to be in his relationship with Jesus. It's not necessarily true that a theologically insightful leader is spiritually mature. Ministry effectiveness is not to be confused with cleanness of heart. What you know about the public persona of a leader does not mean you do not need to be concerned about his private life.

Assumptions that a leadership community makes about the spiritual condition of its leaders, assumptions that allow the community to be passive rather than pastoral, result in a shocked and unprepared community when a fellow leader falls in some way and needs restorative care. If the sin of a leader is revealed to the leadership community that surrounds him, it is because God loves that leader and wants it to be revealed. He has placed that leader in an intimate community of faith, and he has revealed that sin so that the community can function as his arm of convicting and restoring grace. Every leadership community has moments when they are called to be agents of God's restoring mercy. This calling comes in small, private moments as well as in huge, public, and dramatic moments.

If you've made unbiblical assumptions, you are unprepared for these moments of ministry, and they quickly morph into panic and/or anger, punishment, and separation. It has been sad to see, in the face of a leader's fall, how many leadership communities respond in one of two ways, neither restorative.

In the first way, a leadership community, in their inability to believe what has been revealed about a leader they thought they knew and could trust, rises almost immediately to the leader's defense. They minimize or outright discount what has been revealed while they claim to know this leader and are sure that he would never do what he is charged with doing. They go on to publicly proclaim their loyalty to the leader under charge and question the validity of the charges and the motives of those who have come forward with information. The result is that the leader does not get the convicting and restorative care he needs from the community of grace that surrounds him. Even worse, the sin that has gripped his heart and begun to control his life is given room to grow even deeper roots and take a firmer hold. If you have paid attention to the wider ministry leadership community in the last decade, you've seen it happen again and again.

In the second way, the leadership group is again unprepared for God-given moments of restorative calling. In their shock over what has happened, they feel deceived and duped. Compassion for the one caught in sin is replaced by anger. Pastoral care gives way to adversarial responses, which are more punitive than pastoral. They quickly share details publicly that should've never been shared and that could or will harm their fellow leader and his family. They soon break relationship with the leader, and because they have, their communications with him are now legal rather than pastoral. He is no longer considered a part of their leadership community, so they negotiate some kind of severance package and move on.

Don't misunderstand me here; I am not arguing that there aren't times when a leadership community must separate from a fallen and recalcitrant leader, but I am arguing that this should happen at the end of a wholehearted, gospel-saturated attempt at restoration to the church body, even if it means the relinquishing of his position of leadership and authority. The sad thing about the two typical responses I have shared is that they lack preparedness for and commitment to any kind of practical, pastoral, restorative agenda. When a leader has fallen or is facing charges of some kind, and I get the call, I have on many occasions received surprised and sometimes angry responses from the leadership community when I have laid out for them what it looks like to be committed to biblical restoration.

Let me say again: if sin still remains, and it does, then every leadership community needs to be committed to and prepared for restoration.

A RESTORATION NARRATIVE

Here's the last chapter first: every leadership community should commit to representing, in their leadership culture and relationships, the restorative heart of the Redeemer. There are few places where we see more of the zeal of the Lord to restore a wayward leader than in the narrative of Jonah. I want to take some time with you to reflect on what we learn of God's heart there.

Although you surely know the story well, I am going to embed passages from Jonah in our discussion to remind you of Jonah's heart and the heart of his Lord.

> Now the word of the LORD came to Jonah the son of Amittai, saying, "Arise, go to Nineveh, that great city, and call out against it, for their evil has come up before me." But Jonah rose to flee to Tarshish from the presence of the LORD. He went down to Joppa and found a ship going to Tarshish. So he paid the fare

and went down into it, to go with them to Tarshish, away from the presence of the LORD. (Jonah 1:1–3)

Talk about rebelling against the plan and call of the Lord—could there be a clearer example than Jonah? His response to God's call is to turn and go to the other side of the known world. Our window into Jonah's heart is that he has actually bought into the delusion that he can run from the presence of the Lord. If we think it's possible to escape God's presence, we have gone spiritually insane! Jonah is called to be a minister of the gospel. "The gospel?" you may ask. Yes, if you are called to give a message of warning, you are called to represent the Lord's willingness to give people an opportunity to listen, examine, confess, and turn. This is gospel work. If all God wanted to do was judge people, he wouldn't warn them first. God's warning is a beautiful aspect of his grace. Remember, the way the gospel works is that we have to hear the bad news before the good news will mean anything to us.

But Jonah doesn't want to go to a hard place or communicate a hard message to people he doesn't know in a culture he doesn't understand or respect. So he runs from God and his call. Jonah is a rebel and a fool, but he doesn't know it. Now, if I had been in charge, the book of Jonah would have been very short—two verses, to be exact: "Jonah, you run from me, you're done. It's not like I have a shortage of prophets." But I am willing to confess that my response doesn't reflect the heart and way of my Lord.

We get the first hint at the restorative agenda of the Redeemer with three words in verse 4: "But the LORD." These are three of the most important words ever written. They picture God's rescuing, protecting, and restorative agenda. Here is a picture of the beauty and essentiality of the divine interruption. But this interruption happens not because of God's righteous judgment but because of his patient grace. Jonah doesn't know it yet, but he is about to be called back not just to the location to which God called him but also to the Lord who called him.

It is important to understand that the drama about to take place, which gives us a window into the magnitude of the sovereign power of God, is the drama of restoration. God sends a great wind, so great that it terrifies seasoned sailors. To understand why this difficulty has come upon them in desperation, the sailors cast lots, which fall on Jonah. So they ask him who he is and what he has done. Pay careful attention to Jonah's response. He answers, "I am a Hebrew, and I fear the Lord, the God of heaven" (Jonah 1:9). Jonah's identity statement is interesting. By cultural identity he is a God fearer, but in terms of his response to God's call, he doesn't act like someone who fears the Lord. In this way, his words confront us with the difference that may exist in a leader between his confessional theology and his functional theology. Every leadership community needs to be committed to restoration for this very reason. There is often a subtle and progressive separation that takes place in the life and ministry of a leader between his formal confession and the manner by which he lives his life and conducts himself in ministry. The possibility of this drift should be a concern to every leadership community. Pay attention to what the Redeemer, in his sovereignty, is organizing for Jonah:

> So they picked up Jonah and hurled him into the sea, and the sea ceased from its raging. Then the men feared the Lord exceedingly, and they offered a sacrifice to the Lord and made vows.
>
> And the Lord appointed a great fish to swallow up Jonah. And Jonah was in the belly of the fish three days and three nights.
>
> Then Jonah prayed to the Lord his God from the belly of the fish. (Jonah 1:15–2:1)

Yes, God had not abandoned Jonah or his plans for him. Now, you would think, if you didn't know the whole story, that this was the end. Jonah was thrown into the raging sea—God in his righteousness had given Jonah what he deserved—but this was not the end. God appointed a fish to swallow Jonah. Think of the words "appointed a fish." This is the incredible extent of the authority of the Lord. He has the power to appoint a fish as a tool in his restoration of a wayward prophet. Because everything lives under his rule, God uses whatever is necessary to accomplish whatever he intends in the life of those he has called to represent him.

You can see that some kind of turning took place in Jonah, because the man who was so intent on escaping God's presence began praying to the very one he was hoping to escape. In the verses that follow, we can eavesdrop on that deep-sea prayer and get a window into Jonah's heart. Verse 10 clues us in to what God had in mind for Jonah through his appointed instrument, the fish: "The LORD spoke to the fish, and it vomited Jonah out upon the dry land." Yes, it is true: sometimes restorative grace looks like vomit! Restorative grace doesn't always look nice and attractive or feel warm and affirming but, rather, is uncomfortable and hard.

The Jonah narrative preaches to us the heart of restoration. Restoration is much deeper and more foundational than doing what is necessary to quickly get a leader back into his ministry position. Surely Jonah needed much more than that, as the rest of the story makes clear. The heart of God's restorative grace is his zeal to rescue us from us. Jonah needed more than a rescue from the storm, the fish, or the people of Nineveh. Jonah's problem was Jonah, so to be restored to God and his call, Jonah needed to be free from his bondage to himself.

I love the first verse of Jonah 3. I find it deeply encouraging and hope giving. It also gives me insight into an aspect of the heart of God that I am called to represent in my relationship with and ministry to fellow leaders: "Then the word of the LORD came to Jonah the second time." Here's what restoration is about—fresh starts and new beginnings. Between the "already" and the "not yet," it's what the gospel of God's grace offers every ministry leader. It's amazing that God's call would come to Jonah, or to us, even once, but in the face of our foolishness, rebellion, and wandering, it is incredible that it would even come to us a second time. That God can see into our selfish and fickle hearts and still choose to use us is amazing. Jonah the runner has become Jonah the preacher. Jonah, who ran as far as he could from Nineveh, afterward walked its streets proclaiming God's message, and the results were beautiful.

It's here that we might think we are finally at the end of the story and God's work of restoring grace, but we aren't. Let's consider Jonah's reaction to the repentance of Nineveh:

> But it displeased Jonah exceedingly, and he was angry. And he prayed to the LORD and said, "O LORD, is not this what I said when I was yet in my country? That is why I made haste to flee to Tarshish; for I knew that you are a gracious God and merciful, slow to anger and abounding in steadfast love, and relenting from disaster. Therefore now, O LORD, please take my life from me, for it is better for me to die than to live." (Jonah 4:1–3)

Jonah's anger and his question of the wisdom of God's response to Nineveh alert us to the reality that although Jonah had been restored to his ministry calling, he wasn't yet fully restored at the level of his heart. When he should have been humbled and encouraged by the power and presence of God's grace, he was angry at the gift of grace to people he didn't think deserved it. Jonah was mad— so mad that he wanted to die. We are confronted here with the fact that the restoration of a leader cannot just be formal, situational, or locational but must always be heart deep. Restoration that isn't heart deep sets up that leader and his community for further problems because the core of the problem, the leader's heart, has not been restored to where God designed it to be.

What happened next is as important, insight giving, and agenda setting as any other portion of the Jonah narrative:

> Jonah went out of the city and sat to the east of the city and made a booth for himself there. He sat under it in the shade, till he should see what would become of the city. Now the LORD God appointed a plant and made it come up over Jonah, that it might be a shade over his head, to save him from his discomfort. So Jonah was exceedingly glad because of the plant. But when dawn came up the next day, God appointed a worm that attacked the plant, so that it withered. When the sun rose, God appointed a scorching east wind, and the sun beat down on the head of Jonah so that he was faint. And he asked that he might die and said, "It is better for me to die than to live." But God said to Jonah, "Do you do well to be angry for the plant?" And he said, "Yes, I do well to be angry, angry enough to die." And the LORD said, "You pity the plant, for which you did not labor, nor did you make it grow, which came into being in a night and perished in a night. And should not I pity Nineveh, that great city, in which there are more than 120,000 persons who do not know their right hand from their left, and also much cattle?" (Jonah 4:5–11)

God, knowing that Jonah still needed heart restoration work, set up a physical illustration to expose Jonah's heart. Jonah's response to God's grace wasn't amazement and gratitude; no, it was anger. He was mad that mercy was being extended to a group of people he believed didn't deserve it. At the level of his heart, Jonah was completely out of step with God's message, his methods, and his character. This means that even though Jonah finally went where God told him to go and did what God told him to do, in his heart he had abandoned his ambassadorial calling. We should not assume that because a leader is still doing his assigned ministry duties that he is spiritually where God wants him to be.

Now, we might think this would be it for Jonah, that God had finally had enough of Jonah's resistance and anger. But as Jonah was outside the city pouting, God was still working to restore him, once more using creation as his tool. Notice that Jonah is a book without an end, because as Jonah was still resisting and angry, God was still meeting him with restorative grace. Jonah doesn't end with a summary or a conclusion; it ends with a question. It is a question by a patient and gracious Lord that was intended to give Jonah insight into his heart, leading him to confession and repentance.

My prayer is that every ministry leadership community would model the restorative heart of the Lord. Restoration never minimizes the damaging reality of sin, but while it takes sin seriously, it also believes in the power of restorative grace. It believes in God's power to turn a heart and rebuild a life. Restoration isn't motivated by seeing how fast we can get a leader back into the ministry saddle; it's longing that the lapsed leader would know spiritual health of heart and life. Restoration is not about turning away from a ministry leader, even if he needs to be removed from his position and ministry duties, but turning toward him with grace that takes both sin and restoration seriously. Restoration is but another area in which we are called as leaders to take our ambassadorial calling seriously.

No leader is impervious to temptations, because no leader is sin-free and sanctification-finished. Not one. Leaders are susceptible to spiritual blindness. Leaders don't always share God's heart. Leaders don't always find joy in what God has called them to do. Leaders can have bad attitudes and can hide secret sins. Leaders are not always submissive to the Lord they have been called to serve. Leaders don't always treat people with the same grace that God has extended to them. Leaders are capable of losing their way. It is lovingly and graciously protective to take sin seriously in the life of a leader and to remember that ministry is spiritual war. So every leadership community needs to be committed to, and prepared for, those sad and difficult moments when the Savior they serve calls them to a restorative agenda. We cannot be so protective of the institution, the church, that we discard leaders and members of the church as if they're broken and no-longer-needed commodities. I am very aware that there is so much to think about when it comes to the specific plans and process of restoration, so I have committed myself to write a book on that topic.

May every leadership community represent the heart of the Lord that is so beautifully portrayed for us in the book of Jonah. And may we remember, with honesty and humility of heart, that the grace we extend to others is always the grace we also need ourselves. May our hearts be filled with gratitude as we consider that we have all been restored by God's grace, we are all being restored right now by that same grace, and we all will be finally restored by one who will not quit until his restorative mercies have completely rebuilt us into his own image. And may that gratitude of heart shape our response to fellow leaders when sin rears its ugly head.

PRINCIPLE 11

*For church leaders, ministry longevity is always
the result of gospel community.*

— 11.—

LONGEVITY

THE WORDS WERE SPOKEN to me when I was fearful, discouraged, tired, and feeling otherwise beaten down. I didn't want anybody to talk to me. I was a failure, and I was running. I couldn't imagine a life of pastoral leadership anymore. It had once been a passion, a dream that seemed too good to be true, but the passion had morphed into a burden, one I no longer wanted to bear. I had found a safe landing place and couldn't wait to put ministry behind and land there. I had made my announcement, and my heart had already closed to the present and opened up to what was ahead. I had had all of the tough conversations I thought I needed to have. I was done and didn't want to have another awkward, quasi-judgmental encounter.

When he approached me, I hoped it would be a quick, "Hello, we're praying for you," but it was more, so much more. He said, "Paul, we know you're immature, but we haven't asked you to leave." Then he said, "Where is the church going to get mature leaders, if immature leaders run? Don't go." I was frozen for a moment at the power of his words. They were gospel words, and I knew it. They were packed with years of patient wisdom. I think his words were much wiser than even he knew. Packed in that brief sentence was the truth that the key to ministry-leadership effectiveness is longevity. Gospel seeds need time to mature and grow, and the key to longevity is spiritual maturity, because weeding and watering the garden that is the church is such hard work.

I knew instantly that I couldn't and wouldn't run. I un-resigned, if there is such a thing, and stayed for many more years. If you're close to me, you've heard me share this story before, because it was and is so profoundly influential. I was the leader, but I needed to be led. I was the pastor, but I needed to be pastored. I was the primary gospel spokesman, but I needed to have the gospel preached to me. It came powerfully and effectively, a swift wind of the Spirit that I could not push against. It came as the wise words of my Father, which I knew I should not resist. It came as the gentle welcome of my Savior to run to him and not away from him in my angst. But it was little more than one sentence that forever changed the course of my life and ministry. One sentence, courageously and timely spoken, by one man to another one afternoon, but it changed everything.

You see, every leadership community needs to understand that there is no such thing as individual ministry. Every leader's ministry is a community project. Every leader needs the ministry of other leaders in order to grow to the kind of maturity that will allow him to lead well over the long term and end well. Every leader needs leaders who will stand in his way when he is about to choose the wrong way. Every leader needs other leaders to speak truth to him when he can't seem to speak those truths to himself. Every leader, in order to lead long and well, needs fellow leaders to help him see sin that he is too blind to see if left alone. Longevity is the fruit of spiritual maturity, and spiritual maturity is the result of longevity, and both are the fruit of gospel community.

I love the longevity word picture in Isaiah 61:1–3:

The Spirit of the LORD God is upon me,
    because the LORD has anointed me
to bring good news to the poor;
    he has sent me to bind up the brokenhearted,
to proclaim liberty to the captives,
    and the opening of the prison to those who are bound;
to proclaim the year of the LORD's favor,
    and the day of vengeance of our God;
    to comfort all who mourn;
to grant to those who mourn in Zion—
    to give them a beautiful headdress instead of ashes,
the oil of gladness instead of mourning,
    the garment of praise instead of a faint spirit;
that they may be called oaks of righteousness,
    the planting of the LORD, that he may be glorified.

What a beautiful and provocative word picture. What is the gospel good news to the poor? That they will be "oaks of righteousness." Why is an oak tree tall and strong? The answer is longevity. Oak trees are powerful and majestic because they have weathered years and years of withering sun, gusting winds, and bitter cold. Year by year, season by season, they grow in strength. Year by year and season by season they send their roots deeper and deeper into the nutrient soil until they are virtually unmovable. It takes dense wood, hard bark, and deep roots to weather the harsh conditions that an oak tree must weather to be around for generations, but it takes generations for the wood, bark, and roots to grow. If this is a picture of long-term spiritual sturdiness that is God's plan for all of his children, how much more is it needed for ministry leaders?

At the base and in the moist shadows of an oak tree you'll often find mushrooms. Their characteristics are the polar opposite of the oak trees they briefly look up to. Mushrooms grow up overnight and are quickly gone. They aren't strong and have no deep roots.

You can reach down and flick one over with your finger. Big, rapid, short-lived growth is not what God is after; that's why he chose the oak tree and not the mushroom for his word picture. He is after oak trees, long-term spiritual maturity, not just for our eternal good but also for the never-ending display of his glory.

So every ministry leadership community should value and plan for longevity, which means every ministry leadership community must value and plan for spiritual maturity. Every leader needs to continue to mature so he can stand strong in the gusts of wind, driving rain, and cold snows of ministry. No leader should be considered as mature as he or she needs to be. No one. Every leader should long to last and know that spiritual maturity is the key to lasting long. Every leadership community should be clear that giftedness is not the same as spiritual maturity. Biblical literacy is not the same as spiritual maturity. We need to be clear that theological acumen is not the same as spiritual maturity. Ministry success is not the same as spiritual maturity. Popularity is not the same as spiritual maturity. Strategic insight is not the same as spiritual maturity. God is working to produce oaks of righteousness, so every leadership community should be working to produce the same in each of its members.

I had been doing ministry for a long time in a variety of ministry leadership positions, but I felt that it was just about impossible to go on. I felt as if I had been blindsided, caught unaware and unprepared. Life seemed out of control, and the future seemed cloudy at best. I felt afraid, as well as weak and unable, for the first time in a long time. I felt alone, without words to describe to others what I was going through. I no longer jumped out of bed in anticipation; I groaned my way out. I didn't anticipate the ministry opportunities of the day; I dreaded them, overwhelmed by their size and my weakness. I wanted to turn back the clock to when I felt stronger and more ready. But the clock would never turn back, and I would never know the strength I once had. God had another plan, which I struggled with even more than my physical weakness. It was a physical battle but more importantly also a deeply spiritual battle. In order to continue, I needed more than personal resolve; I needed vibrant, loving, courageous, faithful, biblical community. God blessed me with that community. Fellow leaders met me in my weakness, confronted me in my doubt, and comforted me in my suffering. As much as I struggled, I knew that I was not struggling alone. God makes his invisible presence visible through people who are present when the comfort of his presence is needed. God sends his loving words of warning to a leader through fellow leaders who are willing to confront and protect. God makes his invisible comfort visible through agents of comfort he sends where comfort is needed. Gospel community is intended by God to be incarnational, where we are to one another the look on God's face, the touch of his hands, his words, and his presence.

Every leader who becomes an oak of righteousness will weather harsh storms of life and ministry. Perhaps it will be a crushing ministry failure, or the heartbreaking rebellion of a child, or a ministry betrayal, or a battle with an area of sin, or a debilitating church controversy, or a physical illness, or financial distress, or the death of a loved one, or a passage of spiritual discouragement, or an attack on his character or qualifications, but every leader will face storms of some kind. Too many leaders are knocked over by the storms of life in this fallen world. Too many leaders leave ministry fallen or broken in some way. Too many leaders have short-term ministries. Too many leaders fail to experience the joyful fruitfulness of ministry longevity. And let me say here that ministry longevity is not just about hanging in there for a long time but about growing in maturity, and because there is growth in maturity, there is an increasing harvest of long-term fruit. It's more than endurance; it's endurance that produces lasting gospel fruit.

I've already hinted at it but want to clearly address the question here: "Why is leadership longevity so vitally important?" I am deeply persuaded that the church of Jesus Christ has been way too influenced by the *short attention span, next best thing, instant gratification,* and *easily bored* culture of the society in which we live and do our work. We are tempted to chase the next big worship phase and pay too much attention to the next hot young leader; we are too influenced by social media flashes, too interested in strategies for quick results and success, and too willing to search for the key to this or that that would launch our ministries into a different stratum. We are tempted to like quick and despise slow. We are tempted to esteem new and disrespect old. We are attracted to new ideas instead of ancient truths. We are tempted to search for new and better ways instead of old tried-and-true ways. We are tempted to focus on the moment instead of on our potential legacy. The culture around us tends to lack patience and an esteem for long-term process, and I'm afraid we've begun to lack patience too.

You could argue that there are few more important spiritual qualities for a ministry leader than patience. First, you live in a broken world where everything is made more difficult by its dysfunction. You also minister to and lead people who don't always follow well, are easily distracted and daily tempted, and often lose their way. Along with these, you and the people you lead are buffeted, sometimes in life-altering ways, with the storms of life. Finally, and this is most important, you are called to be an ambassador of one who is infinitely patient and has decided that lasting change is most often a process and not an event. Justification, which is a radical life-altering event, is also the first stage in a long-term process of personal heart and life transformation.

How could we not be blown away by God's patience as we matriculate our way through the grand redemptive story? How could we not be amazed by the thousands of years between the fall in

Eden and the victory of the empty tomb? How could we not notice God's willingness to send prophet after prophet after prophet with essentially the same warning and welcome? How could we not take notice of the amazing patience of Jesus with his disciples or with the dysfunctional churches of the Epistles? How could we not be comforted by the fact that in patience God's judgment still waits while his mercy works? How could we miss the fact that our daily hope is connected to our Savior's patient grace? Both the meta story in the Bible and our individual stories are portraits of an ever-faithful and patient Redeemer.

There would be no kingdom of God, no church of Jesus Christ, no people of God, and no population in the new heavens and the new earth if it were not for the infinite patience of the Lord. God is patient in love, judgment, sovereignty, wisdom, power, and mercy. He is willing to do the same thing in you and for you again and again until it takes root and flourishes. He is willing to say the same thing to you over and over again until you hear and live it. He greets your weakness with patience and not disgust. He responds to your wanderings with the patience of rescuing grace and not with condemnation. He patiently picks you up when you fall. He patiently dresses your self-inflicted wounds. He patiently stands in your way when you want your own way. He never tires of you. He never turns his back on you and walks away. He patiently gives himself to the work that he has begun in you, and he will patiently continue until his work is done. His work is a process, not an event. Redemption is longevity work. Redemption is legacy work. Redemption takes patience.

So if any leader in any leadership community is going to become spiritually mature so that he can experience the fruitfulness of ministry longevity, he must be blessed by a gospel community of leaders who patiently work for and contribute to his maturity. This community must not panic when his immaturity is exposed, when his spiritual weaknesses are revealed, when he is more defensive than he should be, more self-assured than is appropriate, when he loses his way for a moment, when he wants to run away, or when he fails in some way. Yes, there are moments when a rebellious and recalcitrant leader who will not submit, confess, and repent must be removed from his leadership position, but whenever this happens, it should be at the end of a long process of patient rescuing, confronting, and restoring grace. Strategizing for ministry longevity means responding with patient grace in the face of a leader's spiritual immaturity, seeking to be part of God's work of rescue and transformation.

SPIRITUALLY MATURE LEADERSHIP: A PORTRAIT

What does a spiritually mature leadership community look like? Consider the beautiful portrait in 2 Corinthians 4:1–18:

> Therefore, having this ministry by the mercy of God, we do not lose heart. But we have renounced disgraceful, underhanded ways. We refuse to practice cunning or to tamper with God's word, but by the open statement of the truth we would commend ourselves to everyone's conscience in the sight of God. And even if our gospel is veiled, it is veiled to those who are perishing. In their case the god of this world has blinded the minds of the unbelievers, to keep them from seeing the light of the gospel of the glory of Christ, who is the image of God. For what we proclaim is not ourselves, but Jesus Christ as Lord, with ourselves as your servants for Jesus' sake. For God, who said, "Let light shine out of darkness," has shone in our hearts to give the light of the knowledge of the glory of God in the face of Jesus Christ.
>
> But we have this treasure in jars of clay, to show that the surpassing power belongs to God and not to us. We are afflicted in every way, but not crushed; perplexed, but not driven to despair;

persecuted, but not forsaken; struck down, but not destroyed; always carrying in the body the death of Jesus, so that the life of Jesus may also be manifested in our bodies. For we who live are always being given over to death for Jesus' sake, so that the life of Jesus also may be manifested in our mortal flesh. So death is at work in us, but life in you.

Since we have the same spirit of faith according to what has been written, "I believed, and so I spoke," we also believe, and so we also speak, knowing that he who raised the Lord Jesus will raise us also with Jesus and bring us with you into his presence. For it is all for your sake, so that as grace extends to more and more people it may increase thanksgiving, to the glory of God.

So we do not lose heart. Though our outer self is wasting away, our inner self is being renewed day by day. For this light momentary affliction is preparing for us an eternal weight of glory beyond all comparison, as we look not to the things that are seen but to the things that are unseen. For the things that are seen are transient, but the things that are unseen are eternal.

I have quoted a rather lengthy passage here because I think Paul's description of the character of his ministry and his own ministry mentality is so important and beautiful. It is a better portrait of the kind of spiritual maturity in a ministry leader that leads to long-term fruitfulness than I could conjure up. Following are three characteristics of his ministry that define spiritual maturity and drive ministry longevity.

Humility

Paul says that there is only one thing that stands as the reason he has this ministry: God's mercy. He says that he has renounced disgraceful, underhanded, and cunning ways. Those attitudes and actions in ministry leadership are never about the success of the gospel, the salvation and growth of others, or the glory of the Savior. They are about a quest for greater personal power, prestige, position, and control. That means they are the fruit of a proud-hearted leader. Paul likens himself to a jar of clay—even more, a cracked jar of clay—one in which the light of the power of God shows through. This word picture is a rebuke to the macho, martial arts–style, strong, aggressive leadership image that is too present in our leadership circles and dents the reputation of the gospel and harms people. Weakness in a ministry leader is not in the way of a vibrant ministry life but is a vital ingredient of it if that weakness causes him to run to God's grace for moment-by-moment help and to be open to the ministry of others. Finally, Paul says he is not at the center of his ministry vision but rather the good of others is his motivation and goal. And he says it "for your sake" (2 Cor. 4:15).

Courage

Paul is courageous in his ministry of the gospel. It is characterized by an "open statement of the truth" (4:2). There is no fear of man or the circumstances that would cause him to compromise the confrontation, comfort, or call of the gospel in any way. Paul has courage in the face of suffering, not living in fear of being destroyed. It does make me wonder how much of what we do as ministry leaders is driven by fear and not by faith. Finally, you see a beautiful picture of what happens when humility is mixed with courage, when Paul says that "we who live are always being given over to death . . . so that the life of Jesus also may be manifested in our mortal flesh" (4:11). Note, this is not a complaint about the hardships of ministry. This is a leader who has died to self and all his desires for comfort and affirmation. The glory of self has been replaced by the glory of Christ, so Paul is willing to endure what would drive many of us out of ministry. But there is more.

Hope

Maybe hope is the most important characteristic of all because of the ground of Paul's hope. It's not in the force of his personality, his ability with words, the sharpness of his mind, his ability to motivate others, the knowledge that he has amassed, or his track record of success. Everything he says about what gives him hope is rooted in the presence, power, promises, and grace of his Redeemer. He has been humbled by the gospel of Jesus Christ, he has courage because of the gospel of Jesus Christ, and he has sturdy hope because of the gospel of Jesus Christ. His hope is rooted in the fact that it is by grace, and grace alone, that he understands the gospel of grace. He says, "God . . . has shone in our hearts to give the light of the knowledge of the glory of God in the face of Jesus Christ" (4:6). Paul talks of how God turns death into life and how he has been blessed with the amazing resources of God's all-surpassing power. He rests in the reality that although he is outwardly wasting away, he is blessed with renewing mercies every day. And he rests in the surety of a glorious destiny that will make this present suffering look light and momentary (4:17).

Spiritual maturity in the life and ministry of a ministry leader is about being humbled by the gospel, made courageous by the gospel, and infused with sturdy hope by the gospel. As leaders we are not naturally humble, courageous, or hopeful. We naturally swing from pride to fear and back again. In order to be what we were designed to be and do what we were called to do as leaders, we need grace, which we are called to protect and proclaim to others, ministered to us in a way that progressively transforms our hearts. This means that in order to lead, we need to be rescued daily from ourselves. As leaders we are not as humble or as courageous or as hopeful as we could be by grace. We all need to grow in greater maturity so that we can experience fruitful longevity, and for this we need faithful, loving gospel community.

STRATEGIZING FOR MINISTRY LEADERSHIP LONGEVITY

So how do you encourage ongoing growth in maturity in the members of your leadership community while also protecting yourself from the temptations of selfism that every ministry leader faces? I want to answer this question by importing a model I've used for a long time. I can think of no newer or better tool to hammer into your leadership culture than this one. It is a model of biblical confrontation. Now, don't be put off by the word *confrontation*. Biblical confrontation is not about pointed fingers, a red face, a loud voice, and accusatory and condemning words. Rather, it is lovingly helping someone see what he is not seeing so that he can own it and grow. Here's how gospel growth works: *you cannot grieve what you do not see, you cannot confess what you haven't grieved, and you can't repent of what you haven't confessed.*

This model of loving, growth-producing confrontation is organized in four parts.

1. *Consideration. What do we need to see, and how can we help our fellow leaders to see it?* Because of the dynamic of spiritual blindness, we don't always see ourselves with accuracy, so we all need instruments of seeing to help us. We must not let ourselves think that we're grace graduates or that no one knows us better than we know ourselves. Because we as leaders have been welcomed by God's grace, we can be humble and approachable, thereby protected and able to grow.

2. *Confession. What thoughts, attitudes, and actions do we need to confess individually and collectively, making humble and honest confession to God and to others when needed?* A ministry leadership community that is growing in grace will be a confessing community. There won't be hidden things in dark closets that we're afraid or too proud to admit. A grace-filled community does not let sin grow and fester. It does not work around questionable circumstances, patterns,

or habits. In a spiritually healthy leadership community, confession isn't unusual and awkward but a regular part of its culture of grace.

3. *Commitment. How is God calling us, individually and as a leadership community, to live out new thoughts, attitudes, words, and actions?* Insight is a step toward change, but it's not change alone. Confession is a further step toward change, but if that confession is not followed by a commitment to a new and more God-honoring way, then it is neither true confession nor change. If confession is the result of eyes that now see and a heart that is grieved, it will be followed by a desire for rescuing and transforming grace. Every leadership community should be constantly pushed forward and matured by fresh commitments to the call of God's grace.

4. *Change. How can we ingrain these new commitments, individually and together, into our routine life and ministry as a leadership community?* We must consider where God is calling us to change the way we operate, the attitudes we have toward one another and those we serve, and the way we relate to one another and those we serve. How is God calling us to change the way we think about and do the "business" of ministry? What changes do we need to make, and how will they be made? We must remember that change hasn't taken place until change has taken place. You don't follow God by talking about following him but by following him in joyful humility and submission. May God meet us with his grace so that we would be not only willing but joyfully doing.

So I have given you a practical model for strategizing the kind of ministry leadership longevity that is only ever the result of a leadership community continuing to grow in spiritual maturity, individually and collectively. And I am filled with hope for every leadership community around the world, because I really do believe in the awesome power of God's rescuing, forgiving, and transforming grace, and that we have been given "all things that pertain to life and godliness" (2 Pet. 1:3). Between the "already" of our conversion and our ministry calling and the "not yet" of our home going, God has already given every one of us everything we need to be what we're supposed to be and to do what we're supposed to do right here, right now. It is the generosity and surety of this gospel of grace that causes me to write with hope. I hope you have hope, too, in a way that infuses you with humility and courage for the long run.

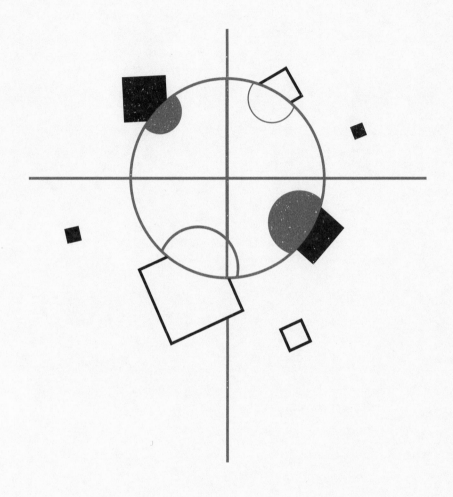

PRINCIPLE 12

You will only handle the inevitable weakness, failure, and sin of your leaders when you view them through the lens of the presence, power, promises, and grace of Jesus.

—12.—

PRESENCE

IT WAS A COUP OF SORTS, done behind my back by people I trusted. I had founded a Christian school, written its philosophy of education, assisted in the design of its curriculum, and hired and led all of its teachers. I had rallied a community around the school who loved it and worked to make it healthy. I was not a perfect leader. I was young and made many mistakes. We did have some facilities issues and financial stresses, but that is not unusual for an independent Christian school. I led a board that seemed unified and ready to address the school's weaknesses. I was very willing to turn the leadership of the school over to another because I knew I could not do what needed to be done there while also serving as a full-time pastor. From my vantage point, the next leader simply wasn't on the horizon.

That Thursday evening the unthinkable happened. In a well-planned move by a group on the board, I was voted out of my position as president of the board and removed from all leadership over the school. I was so shocked and hurt. I'll never forget walking into my house later that night. I must have had a devastated look on my face, because my wife, Luella, asked me what was wrong. I blurted out, "I have been kicked out of the school!" She also couldn't believe what was happening. I had been the school principal for years, without pay, while paying tuition for my children to attend. I didn't know that I had lost the confidence of my fellow leaders. I didn't know that there was so much disunity among us. I didn't know that we would never have a chance to talk about our problems before I would be voted out. I didn't know.

Now, when you go through something like this, bitterness lurks right around the corner, as it did for me. In the days that followed, instead of rehearsing once again the greatness, grace, and presence of my Savior, I repeated to myself over and over again all the wonderful ways I had served this school. With each rehearsal I got more bitter. "Do they have any clue of all the things I have done for them?" I would ask myself again and again. I felt that I had been robbed, as if something that belonged to me had been taken away. The school had been my baby. It was precious to me. It was a valued piece of ministry fruit. I was preaching a false gospel to myself, and I didn't know it. But my Savior was faithful and began to remind me of the true gospel, the one that has him at the center and not me.

Tearfully I began to accept that that school was not mine nor had it ever been. God had given me the vision and gifts that I employed there. God had raised up a community of support. God had provided the resources so we could have a building. God had gifted and connected us to wonderful, dedicated teachers. God had worked insight and commitment into the hearts of parents so they'd be willing to make the sacrifices necessary to send their children to our school. And the children in that school didn't belong to me but to my Lord. Not only had they been created by him to live for his glory, but they had also been chosen by God to be in families of faith, families pursuing a distinctly Christian approach to education.

All that the school was, was the result of God's presence. There was a central leader, present and active at every point, who had led the school to this point, and that leader was not me. There is no way, on the basis of my gifts and ability to lead, that I could have independently produced those results. I do not have the wisdom, power, and control necessary. The school wasn't first a testimony to my insight and hard work but rather to God's presence and grace. I had been improperly removed from the school, but God hadn't. He was still present. It was his school and not mine, and he had the right to do with it whatever he wished.

Along the way, in my work with the school, something had happened to me. I didn't know it had happened until that disastrous evening. In my daily focus on what I could do and should do, how in the world I would do it, who I would do it with, and how it would be funded, I had become a *presence amnesiac*. Here's what I mean. I was so busy being present that I had lost sight of the awesome encouragements and important protections that are only ever found when a leader keeps his eyes focused on the glory of the presence of the Lord.

Bad things happen to a ministry leader and to a leadership community when ministry leadership work so commands focus that they begin to functionally forget the presence of the Lord. I'm not talking about becoming theologically liberal but about the dangerous gap that often begins to grow in ministry leadership between our confessional theology and our functional theology. There are times when what we say we believe doesn't seem to be guiding our actions, reactions, and responses or the state of our emotions. There I was—I hadn't altered one cell of my theology, but I had become self-focused and self-reliant—and what actually belonged to God, I viewed as belonging to me (although if you had asked me, of course I would have said that the school belonged to the Lord). When the school was taken out of my hands, I took an emotional and spiritual header until the Lord met me in his grace and reminded me of the game-changing reality of his presence.

You may have had no experience like that, but if you are a leader of a church or ministry, you are probably focused and busy, and you too may be in danger of being so central to yourself that you too have become a presence amnesiac. Leading a ministry without the presence of the Lord filling the eyes of your heart is dangerous for any leader or leadership community. If it's possible to look at creation and not see the glory and presence of the one who created it all and controls it to this day, then it is also possible to look at your ministry and forget that every good thing there is the work of hands greater than your own.

CASE STUDY I: PRESENCE AND GLORY

As a means of drawing your attention toward the protective power of leaders reminding one another again and again of the right here, right now presence and glory of God, I have decided to use Daniel 4 and Nebuchadnezzar's dream as a case study. Now, I know that the primary gospel message of Daniel is to remind us again that God rules over the affairs of nations and the sweep of human history in order to advance his redemptive plan for our good and his glory. At the same time, it seems important to ask why there is such fine-grain detail in Daniel. Could it be that the detail is there to illustrate once again the fundamental human struggle and the gracious transforming work of God in response to it?

Following is a portion of Daniel 4 (vv. 24–37) as he is interpreting Nebuchadnezzar's confusing dream. I know that this pagan king is in ways totally unlike any ministry leader; on the other hand, there is one place of significant commonality: the temptation to self-glory. It will be there until sin is finally eradicated from our hearts. The core of sin is self-glory. Paul reminds us in 2 Corinthians 5:15 that

Jesus came so that those who live would no longer live for themselves. Nebuchadnezzar stands in Scripture as an extreme example
of what lurks in everyone's heart. In this way, this passage should
expose, convict, and encourage us all. Nebuchadnezzar really is a
man just like us.

> "This is the interpretation, O king: It is a decree of the Most
> High, which has come upon my lord the king, that you shall
> be driven from among men, and your dwelling shall be with
> the beasts of the field. You shall be made to eat grass like an ox,
> and you shall be wet with the dew of heaven, and seven periods
> of time shall pass over you, till you know that the Most High
> rules the kingdom of men and gives it to whom he will. And as
> it was commanded to leave the stump of the roots of the tree,
> your kingdom shall be confirmed for you from the time that you
> know that Heaven rules. Therefore, O king, let my counsel be
> acceptable to you: break off your sins by practicing righteous-
> ness, and your iniquities by showing mercy to the oppressed,
> that there may perhaps be a lengthening of your prosperity."
>
> All this came upon King Nebuchadnezzar. At the end of
> twelve months he was walking on the roof of the royal palace
> of Babylon, and the king answered and said, "Is not this great
> Babylon, which I have built by my mighty power as a royal
> residence and for the glory of my majesty?" While the words
> were still in the king's mouth, there fell a voice from heaven,
> "O King Nebuchadnezzar, to you it is spoken: The kingdom has
> departed from you, and you shall be driven from among men,
> and your dwelling shall be with the beasts of the field. And you
> shall be made to eat grass like an ox, and seven periods of time
> shall pass over you, until you know that the Most High rules the
> kingdom of men and gives it to whom he will." Immediately the
> word was fulfilled against Nebuchadnezzar. He was driven from
> among men and ate grass like an ox, and his body was wet with

the dew of heaven till his hair grew as long as eagles' feathers, and his nails were like birds' claws.

At the end of the days I, Nebuchadnezzar, lifted my eyes to heaven, and my reason returned to me, and I blessed the Most High, and praised and honored him who lives forever,

> for his dominion is an everlasting dominion,
>> and his kingdom endures from generation to
>>> generation;
> all the inhabitants of the earth are accounted as nothing,
>> and he does according to his will among the host of
>>> heaven
>> and among the inhabitants of the earth;
> and none can stay his hand
>> or say to him, "What have you done?"

At the same time my reason returned to me, and for the glory of my kingdom, my majesty and splendor returned to me. My counselors and my lords sought me, and I was established in my kingdom, and still more greatness was added to me. Now I, Nebuchadnezzar, praise and extol and honor the King of heaven, for all his works are right and his ways are just; and those who walk in pride he is able to humble. (Dan. 4:24–37)

There is a warning there that every ministry leadership community needs to hear and constantly consider with watchful eyes. If we are not living with the presence and glory of God always in focus and always as the primary motivator of all we say and do, what we say and do will be driven by the glory of self. Every human being is glory oriented, because that orientation is meant to drive us to God. So we are all always living for some type of glory. It is important to understand that this is one of the primary spiritual battlegrounds of ministry leadership. For ministry leaders, success is more spiritually dangerous than failure, much power rather than no power tempts us to dominate, acclaim is more of a potential spiritual pitfall than rejection, and seasoned experience carries with it more temptation than the unknowns of starting out.

It is vital that we minister and lead with God's presence and glory always in view. If we don't, this passage warns us of three things that will invariably happen. Verse 27 alerts us to the first: "Therefore, O king, . . . break off your sins by practicing righteousness, and your iniquities by showing mercy to the oppressed." If the glorious presence of God does not fill our eyes and rule our heart, we will lead not out of submission to the Lord and love for others but for ourselves and our glory. Notice that the framework of verse 27 is the two great commandments: love God above all else (practice righteousness) and love your neighbor as yourself (show mercy to the oppressed). When, as leaders, we are daily blown away by the presence and glory of God (I'm not talking here about our confessional theology but about our moment-by-moment consciousness), we joyfully do our work inside the boundaries of the two great commandments, laboring for God's glory and the good of others. But if we become presence and glory amnesiacs, our actions will be driven by a very different set of motives.

I have been shocked by the selfism that is regularly accepted in our ministry leadership community, as I have been saddened to see those temptations in my own heart. You can see ministry leadership self-glory in self-aggrandizing Twitter posts, in Instagram photos, and all over Facebook. You see it in the needless demands that speakers regularly make. You see it in pastoral entitlement and impatience. You can see it around the table in regional and national leadership gatherings, where way too much bragging takes place. There is too much confidence in self and self-importance among us. There are times when we are too similar to the disciples arguing about who is going to be the greatest in the kingdom.

We must never quit reminding ourselves of God's presence and glory lest we quit doing what we're doing out of allegiance to him and love for others and do it for ourselves.

Daniel 4:24–37 alerts us to a second danger of losing sight of the presence and glory of God. It is found in verse 30: "Is not this great Babylon, which I have built by my mighty power as a royal residence and for the glory of my majesty?" What a mind-blowing, spiritually delusional statement! There is no way that Nebuchadnezzar was in his position from the independent exercise of his own power. The entire book of Daniel is an argument against such a self-aggrandizing perspective. But the spiritual dynamic here should live as a gracious warning to every ministry leadership community. If we are not doing our work with the presence and glory of God in view, we will take credit for what we could never institute, produce, and control on our own.

We ministry leaders are given way too much credit for the results of our ministry, and we should all resist it. People tend to think that we have way more power and wisdom than we actually have. Ministry success is a testament to who God is and what he is willing to do through us by grace. We have no ability whatsoever to control all the things that need to be controlled for ministry success. We have no control over the gifts we have been given. We have no power to turn the hearts of people to the Lord. We are tools in the hands of one of awesome power, glory, and grace, and nothing more. The gospel institutions we have built have been built by his power and grace, so they stand as monuments to his presence and glory and not to us. As Romans 11:36 so powerfully says, "From him and through him and to him are all things. To him be glory forever. Amen."

There is a third thing in this Daniel passage. It is found in the humiliation of Nebuchadnezzar. If God intended only to bring judgment down on Nebuchadnezzar, there wouldn't have been the dream and its interpretation. The dream and interpretation were God's gracious warnings. Even the harshest of warnings in Scripture are expressions of grace, God giving people one more opportunity to listen, examine, confess, and repent. So the humiliation of Nebuchadnezzar was not judgment but grace. And as he surrendered his glory to the glory of the Lord, his kingship was returned even greater than before.

God will not surrender his glory to another. He is not willing that we take credit for what he alone can do. So he will lead us into those moments when we face the humiliation of our self-glory devastation. Those moments when it all comes crashing down, when sin is exposed or where ministry leadership is taken away, are not judgment but rescuing mercy. We know our judgment was borne by Jesus, so God lays us low because he loves us and is drawing us once again to himself, to live and lead once again inside the wise and loving boundaries he has set for us.

It is vital that every ministry leadership community is bathed over and over again, as a regular part of its ministry culture, in the right here, right now presence and glory of God. This glory-of-God culture is a protection against self-glory and will keep us from taking credit for ministry successes we could never produce on our own.

CASE STUDY 2: PRESENCE AND GRACE

There is another aspect to keeping the presence of God always before your eyes. It is the need for ministry leaders to continue to remind themselves of the inexhaustible resources of protecting and enabling grace that are theirs because the source of that grace has promised to never leave them or forsake them. I want to take you to that moment when the army of Israel is encamped in the Valley of Elah, ready to do battle with the Philistine army. Remember that God had promised this land to the children of Israel and had committed himself to releasing his power to defeat the enemies they would encounter there. This account of the defeat of the giant Philistine warrior stands in Scripture as another reminder that God will not only defend his people but will also allow nothing or no one to get in the way of his grand redemptive plan. At the same time, the way his children interact with his agenda is instructive.

"All the men of Israel, when they saw the man, fled from him and were much afraid" (1 Sam. 17:24). This is the reaction the leaders of the Israelite army had when they first saw Goliath and received his challenge. They were immediately terrified and fled, and they did this for forty days. As you read their response, it should strike you as very wrong. They are terrified not just because Goliath exists but, more foundationally, because they are in the throes of devastating theological amnesia. This is the army of the almighty God, who is with them and for them. No power on earth is able to tell God what to do, stand in his way, or defeat him. The men of Israel are afraid not just because Goliath is big and powerful, but because they are forgetful. When a leader forgets the powerful and gracious presence of the Lord, he also forgets who he is and what is his as God's child. Vertical amnesia always leads to identity confusion.

Because they are forgetful of God's grace—that he would choose them, deliver them from slavery, preserve them in the wilderness, give them a land of milk and honey, and fight their battles for them—they are making the wrong calculations in this moment. The reality is not these normal-sized soldiers against this huge Philistine warrior; it is this puny Philistine against almighty God. Now, who would you predict would win that battle?

David shows up, sent by his father, Jesse, to bring provision to his brothers, and he is immediately bothered by the scene, so he says: "What shall be done for the man who kills this Philistine and takes away the reproach from Israel? For who is this uncircumcised Philistine, that he should defy the armies of the living God?" (17:26).

And David volunteers to go down across that valley and face this fierce warrior.

David doesn't volunteer because he is delusional, has an over-inflated view of his abilities, or because he is full of himself. What he says next lets you know why he has such courage: "Let no man's heart fail because of him. . . . Your servant has struck down both lions and bears, and this uncircumcised Philistine shall be like one of them, for he has defied the armies of the living God" (17:32, 36). From his own experience, David is deeply convinced of the grace of God's presence and power. He is convinced that God keeps his promises. This means David is convinced that God is right there with him in the valley, and that because he is, David will be able to do things in the power of God that he could never do on his own. "The LORD who delivered me from the paw of the lion and from the paw of the bear will deliver me from the hand of this Philistine" (17:37). David is saying, "I've already experienced God's enabling power in moments of danger." His remembrance of the grace of God's presence and power is the sole source of the courage he has in this moment that would bring terror into the hearts of seasoned soldiers. The subsequent defeat of Goliath is a testament not first to David's courage but to the presence of the Lord and the gracious exercise of his power on Israel's behalf.

Perhaps it doesn't need to be said, but I'll say it anyway: effective, long-term ministry leadership takes courage. You will face opposition. You will endure accusations, misunderstandings, and questions about your qualifications. At times precious relationships will be strained and family burdens will weigh you down. Physical illness and weakness might at times make ministry look impossible, and you'll feel weak and unable, not up to the task God has assigned you. The enemy will taunt and tempt. At times your work will bear no visible fruit. You will be tempted to fantasize about an easier place or ministry. There may be times when you feel undervalued and underappreciated. At times you might feel overburdened by trying to balance family ministry with your gospel ministry, and it seems you're not doing either well.

It is the distinct honor of every ministry leader to be an ambassador of the Savior. It should give you joy, make you pinch yourself to make sure it's not a dream, and be the thing that yanks you out of bed in the morning, ready for another day of service. It is wonderful to be called to stand next to the gospel every day of your life and to be a leader in the worldwide movement of the gospel. But it must also be said again that a call to ministry leadership is a call to suffer. Jesus warned the disciples he was leaving behind that they would suffer as he had. Paul says that we have been chosen not only to believe in Christ but also to suffer for him (Phil. 1:29). It is in those difficult, unwanted, and unexpected moments of hardship in the life of a ministry leader that presence amnesia is so debilitating and devastating.

When, as a leader, in a moment of hardship, you forget the grace of God's presence and his commitment to exercise his power for your sake, you are then a sitting duck for the cruel lies of the enemy. He wants you to give way to anxiety-producing "what ifs." He wants you to go back and question your calling. He wants to rob you of your courage and desire to continue. He wants to create chaos inside you and disunity between you and fellow leaders. He will attack as often as he can and take any foothold he is given.

As a ministry leader, you should remind yourself over and over and over again that you do not wrestle against flesh and blood but against spiritual forces in high places. And as you remind yourself of who it is that actually opposes you, you'd better also remind yourself of the presence, glory, and grace of the one who is with you and for you. What every ministry leader will face he cannot endure or defeat on his own, and this is precisely why God has promised that he would not think of leaving you and that forsaking you is simply out of the question. As a ministry leader, God's presence is your hope, God's presence is your confidence, God's presence is your refuge, God's presence is your courage, God's presence calls you to humility and dependency, and God's presence is your constant motivation to continue. Ministry leadership, at its core, is about a community of leaders practicing together the presence of the Lord.

I wrote this book because I love the church of Jesus Christ and have a deep affection for all who have surrendered their lives and gifts to ministry leadership. I love spending time with young leaders. I love encouraging them in their work and warning them of the dangers to come. I love any moment I get to sit with seasoned pastors who have served and suffered with joy. And because my heart is in the church, I am concerned about the spiritual health of the community of leaders that pastor its people and direct its ministries. This book is not about the strategic work of the ministry leadership community but about protecting and preserving its spiritual depth so it may do its work with long-term fruitfulness. Really, this book is about the Lord of the church, about his love for the ambassadors he has called to represent him, and how he meets their every need with glorious and faithful grace. What kind of ministry leadership would I hope this book would stimulate? I'll let the apostle Paul answer:

> Working together with him, then, we appeal to you not to receive the grace of God in vain. For he says,
>
> > "In a favorable time I listened to you,
> > and in a day of salvation I have helped you."
>
> Behold, now is the favorable time; behold, now is the day of salvation. We put no obstacle in anyone's way, so that no fault may be found with our ministry, but as servants of God we commend ourselves in every way: by great endurance, in afflictions, hardships, calamities, beatings, imprisonments, riots, labors,

sleepless nights, hunger; by purity, knowledge, patience, kindness, the Holy Spirit, genuine love; by truthful speech, and the power of God; with the weapons of righteousness for the right hand and for the left; through honor and dishonor, through slander and praise. We are treated as impostors, and yet are true; as unknown, and yet well known; as dying, and behold, we live; as punished, and yet not killed; as sorrowful, yet always rejoicing; as poor, yet making many rich; as having nothing, yet possessing everything.

We have spoken freely to you, Corinthians; our heart is wide open. (2 Cor. 6:1–11)

May God form in your heart the spirit expressed by these words, and may he bless you with every grace you need as you lead in his name.

GENERAL INDEX

humility, 24–25, 74, 108; as defense
    against spiritual attack, 122–23;
    in leadership community, 152;
    and longevity, 201–2, 203, 206

"I Am," 21–22
identity, 162–4, 218
identity in Christ, 156, 164–67
identity exchange, 168–74
identity in ministry, 156, 162,
    167–68, 170
idolatry, 88–90, 109–10
imbalance, 88
impatience, 62, 215
inspection, 26
intercession, 58
interpretation of identity, 162–63
introspection, 16

James, on restoration, 68
jar of clay, 202
Jesus Christ: authority of, 21–22;
    glory of, 202; model of leader-
    ship, 134; as our nurturer, 56;
    presence of, 21–22; as suffering
    servant, 142
job, as identity, 164
Jonah, 28, 183–90
joy, in self-denial, 140–41

kingdom of God, 34, 199

labor life, 78
leaders: become unapproachable and
    controlling, 46, 172; character
    deficiencies in, 105; defined by
    achievement, 38–39; disciple-
    ship of, 84; drift into imbal-
    ance, 95; held accountable to
    protect souls, 27; limits of, 170;
    need confronting and restor-
    ative grace, 113; need grace, 158;
    not impervious to temptation,

189; public fall of, 110; qualities,
    104; regularly confessing faults,
    57; restoration to, 28
leadership community: and achieve-
    ment, 37–38; candor of,
    148–58; change in culture,
    35–36; as confessional com-
    munity, 152–53; conversation
    about spiritual warfare, 124–25;
    as defenders and advocates, 112,
    182; denials of gospel in, 152;
    and fallen leaders, 27, 110; and
    gospel of Jesus, 22–24; healthy,
    18; loving confrontation with
    leaders, 110; must discuss
    balance in lives of leaders, 91;
    relationships in, 155; as restor-
    ative community, 29, 180, 183;
    shepherding pastors, 53; values
    of, 101; weaknesses in, 19–20
lifestyle diseases, 82
limits, 71–84
longevity, 193–206
love: for Jesus, 56; for neighbor, 215;
    for one another, 56
lust, 180

marriage: problems in, 97; self-
    sacrificial love in, 105; unfaith-
    fulness, 181
materialism, 95
maturity, 83–84, 194–96, 197,
    200–203
mercy to the oppressed, 215
ministry: and accountability, 105;
    busyness of, 72, 125; as com-
    munity project, 194; and family,
    79; hardships of, 53; humility
    in, 74; motivations in, 109; and
    private life, 181–82; as source of
    identity, 156, 162, 167–68, 170;
    as spiritual warfare, 56, 115–16;

SCRIPTURE INDEX

Also Available from Paul David Tripp

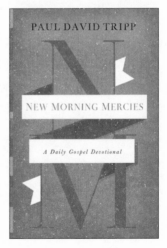

For more information, visit **crossway.org**.

PAUL TRIPP MINISTRIES

Paul Tripp Ministries connects the
transforming power of Jesus Christ to
everyday life through encouraging articles,
videos, sermons, devotionals, and more—
all available online and on social media.

PaulTripp.com

 /pdtripp   @paultripp   @paultrippquotes